The power of the media magni
sound, and print accelerate; the
is limitless. In this highly read
laboration between media and helping professionals to turn the tide of
trauma. It is a must read for anyone concerned with the future peace
and sanity of the world.

—BABETTE ROTHSCHILD, MSW, LCSW
Author of *The Body Remembers:*
The Psychophysiology of Trauma and Trauma Treatment

The beauty of this book is that it shows a way for the media to use their
huge influence in helping ways; it does not join the simple critics who
are inclined to "kill the messenger." This book is a must for journalists,
cameramen, producers, and everyone in the media business, but basically
for everyone who is interested in the role of the media on trauma.

—DANNY BROM
Co-author of *Coping with Trauma* and co-founder
and director of the Israeli Trauma Center in Jerusalem

Since September 11, the oft-neglected issue of trauma and its aftermath
has gained national attention. In this well-researched and very read-
able book, Gina Ross makes an invaluable contribution to an issue that
affects every one of us, either directly or indirectly.

Ross explains how past traumas haunt and debilitate us in myriad
ways, long after the events themselves have passed. She shows us how
many of our current problems, from war to poverty, addiction to child-
abuse, perpetuate this vicious cycle, as victims become aggressors. Only
in understanding the roots of unconscious, trauma-based behavior, and
then by enacting a healing process, can such cycles be broken.

In a unique exploration of the nature and healing of trauma, **Beyond**
the Trauma Vortex *gives us the tools to shift centuries of human suf-*
fering toward a new way of seeing, feeling, and being in the world. The
result can be a happier, more productive society, one that perpetuates
positive rather than negative cycles, and where altruism overcomes self-
ishness, respect prevails over abuse, love conquers fear, and the nobler
instincts of humankind can truly manifest.

—HYLA CASS, M.D.
Assistant Clinical Professor of Psychiatry, UCLA School of Medicine,
and author of *St. John's Wort: Nature's Blues Buster, and Natural Highs*

BEYOND
THE
TRAUMA VORTEX

THE MEDIA'S ROLE IN HEALING
FEAR, TERROR, AND VIOLENCE

GINA ROSS

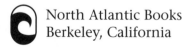

North Atlantic Books
Berkeley, California

Published by
North Atlantic Books
P.O. Box 12327
Berkeley, California 94712

International Trauma-Healing Institute
269 S. Lorraine Blvd
Los Angeles, CA 90004

Cover photographs by Rizwana and David Goldman
Cover design by Rizwana
Book design by Jan Camp

Printed in the United States of America

Beyond the Trauma Vortex is sponsored by the Society for the Study of Native Arts and Sciences, a nonprofit educational corporation whose goals are to develop an educational and crosscultural perspective linking various scientific, social, and artistic fields; to nurture a holistic view of arts, sciences, humanities, and healing; and to publish and distribute literature on the relationship of mind, body, and nature.

North Atlantic Books' publications are available through most bookstores. For further information, call 800-337-2665 or visit our website at www.northatlanticbooks.com.

Substantial discounts on bulk quantities are available to corporations, professional associations, and other organizations. For details and discount information, contact our special sales department.

Library of Congress Cataloging-in-Publication Data

Ross, Gina. 1947–
Beyond the Trauma Vortex: The Media's Role in Healing Fear, Terror, and Violence / by Gina Ross; foreword by Peter A. Levine.
    p. cm.
Includes bibliographical references.
    ISBN 1-55643-446-4 (pbk.)
    1. Disasters—Press coverage. 2. Violence—Press coverage.
3. War—Press coverage. 4. Psychic trauma. I. Title.
PN4784.D57 R67 2003
303.6—dc21

2002152455
CIP

1 2 3 4 5 6 7 8 9 DATA 08 07 06 05 04 03

TABLE OF CONTENTS

The function of the soul is to indicate its desire, not impose it.
The function of the mind is to CHOOSE from its alternatives.
The function of the body is to act out THAT CHOICE.
When body, mind, and soul create together in harmony and in
  unity—God is made flesh.

—Neale Donald Walsch
Author of *Conversations With God*

FOREWORD

The media does more than report news. Particularly since the events of September 11, it has, in dramatic and subtle ways, influenced the reaction of the American public to those events. For better or for worse the media has an effect not only in informing—but on *how* that information affects the public.

President Bush has asked Americans not to panic—to be alert, but not anxious. The media, to a significant degree, will have an important role in determining whether we will remain stable and actively mobilized or whether we will fall prey to helpless fear and resignation. Never before have the media had such an important role in society. This will be particularly true in the event that "sleeper" terrorist cells further attack us. Let us remember that the goal of terrorism is not primarily to destroy, kill, or damage but rather to terrorize and demoralize the populace. It is to demoralize us so that we lose our capacity for pleasure and productive work.

This is the first time we have been attacked on our own soil since the revolutionary and civil wars. With coverage reaching virtually the entire nation almost instantly, the role of the media may prove to be critical as to how we hold together as a nation. With this high level of responsibility—and with the media itself already a target of terrorism—media persons, like most people, have little understanding or tools for dealing with the effects of trauma.

Gina Ross has come along at the right moment to help meet this critical need. In this book she deftly lays out an accessible understanding of trauma and describes simple guidelines that media personnel can use to help resource themselves and their audiences in the prevention of panic. If the media accepts this new role it will help us come together not only as a nation but as a people as well. This is a book for our times.

—Peter A. Levine, author of *Waking the Tiger*

ACKNOWLEDGMENTS

I have much to be thankful for. Writing this book is one of many gifts I have received in life. It afforded me the opportunity to meet wonderful and generous people. It has directed my exploration in the field of trauma, a field that frightened me at first; but as I kept opening the doors of its secrets, both my inner and outer life was very enriched. There are many I want to thank for helping me along this journey.

This book would not have been possible without Lori Milken. While talking about my Trauma Healing Project for Israel and Palestine over lunch with Lori and her brother Ed Newman, I happened to mention my thoughts about the significant role the media can play in the healing of trauma. Keenly interested in the subject herself, she challenged and helped me turn my thoughts into reality. Her generous offer to underwrite and edit this book and her support along the way made my dream possible.

Terrence MacNally was instrumental in doing the original research and writing the first draft. His knowledge of the media world and his familiarity with psychology and trauma made him the ideal person for pulling the initial effort together. Thank you to David Goldman for contributing cover photos. Please visit his website at www.davidgoldman.com.

Lanie Abrams, an art therapist and writer friend in Northern California, edited several chapters. She joined my endeavor with passion and never fatigued in the editing and re-editing process.

Peter Levine, author of *Waking the Tiger*, creator of the Somatic Method, as well as my friend and teacher, was instrumental in sparking my interest in the subject of trauma as a root cause of

violence and ethnic wars. The work and friendship of Dr. Bessel
van der Kolk, author of *Traumatic Stress,* supplied the research on
the costs of trauma, and informed my understanding of its impact
on society.

I am indebted to Charles Figley for his accessibility as well as
his work on "compassion fatigue," a crucial concept for understanding journalists. To Frank Ochberg, for his artful guidance in
approaching media members as friends rather than adversaries.
Frank's development of a Trauma and Journalism course, and the
Dart Center, set a tone for this book. I was influenced as well by
Roger Simpson, author of *Covering Violence.* His research on PTSD
in journalists is groundbreaking and inspirational.

Thank you to Dr. Danny Brom, my "partner-in-crime" for the
last four years, my co-creator of the International Trauma Conference organized in Jerusalem and Gaza in 1999, and co-founder
and Director of the Israel Trauma Center in Jerusalem. Co-author
with Kleber of *Coping with Trauma,* he is an expert in the research
of trauma; to Dr. Dave Gross, my generous psychiatrist friend from
Florida and co-presenter in my first media workshop in Israel; to
Steve Shwartz, Director of Public Relations at Herzog Hospital in
Jerusalem for his perspicacity and ability to grasp large concepts.

Thank you to my friend Ido Aharoni, former Israeli consul for
Communications in Los Angeles, currently the Israeli consul of
Media and Public Relations in New York. He understood the
poignant need to use the knowledge of the trauma, mediation,
and cross-cultural psychology at the political level; he helped me
make the contacts I needed. My thanks to Rabbi Abraham Cooper
from the Wiesenthal Center in Los Angeles for his support and
his offer to disseminate the work.

My thanks to my friends in Israel, Yona Shahar-Levy, Ofra
Ayalon, Robin Twite, Sharon Rosen, and Danny Kropf. And to
professional friends and colleagues—my longtime friend Hyla

Cass, a great connector; Liana and Jack Kornfield, Yaël Danielli, and Babette Rotschild, all authors in their own right; Pina Di Cola, Doris El Tawil Cohen, Darling Villena Mata, David Grill, Kerry Cheek, and Vivian Gold and her husband Phil for their ongoing support and feedback.

And hats off to journalists—to Stephanie Du Bois, the first journalist to encourage the idea of an appeal to the media to take on a sizable role in the healing of trauma. And my heartfelt thanks to Akila Gibbs for her candid conversations with me about her life as a journalist, and for allowing me to tell her story in the book. I met Akila through the insightful connecting ability of my dear friend Susan Brown, a solid supporter and avid listener of this project. My thanks to Sherry Ricciardi, a passionate journalist working with trauma in war zones, for her insightful advice on journalistic values and her article, heavily quoted in the book; and to Migael Sherer, journalist and writer, very knowledgeable about trauma, for her generous editing and support, as well as to former CNN Chief Editor in Beirut, Jerry Levin, for his insightful editing of several chapters.

I would also like to thank all of my family: My mother Frida Hamoui for her unshakable belief in me and her encouragement to be the most and the best of who I am; my sisters, Monda and Vivo, as well as my brothers, Joe and Solly Hamoui, for their support and for accepting graciously that I spent less time with them in Brazil for the last three years. My brother Elio, for always being available to help, and my twin sister Rina and sister Arlette, for believing in and encouraging what I was doing, no matter how impossible it seemed.

I am ever so grateful to my children Eric and Jenny Ross for their love, constant encouragement, and acceptance of my seeming absent-mindedness in the last couple of years. Jenny did much typing and re-typing of the book.

No matter how much help I got along the way, it is my dear husband Reg Wilson, constantly pushing me to grow into larger shoes, who encouraged and challenged me to undertake the writing of this book, the monumental effort of bringing trauma out of the closet and spreading a hopeful message: That even as trauma is contagious, awareness of trauma dynamics can cause the healing of trauma to be more contagious. He saw no task too difficult for me to undertake and with much generosity and sacrifice gave up some of the romantic time we had planned together.

INTRODUCTION

"Trauma is at the root of violence." During a training I attended in Somatic Experiencing, given by Dr. Peter A. Levine in 1994, this sentence rang through my being. It was to direct my professional efforts for the next eight years. Once I understood the tremendous impact of trauma, I was called to action. I learned how trauma haunts and debilitates its victims, even long after the events themselves have passed. I learned how much of humanity's suffering inadvertently perpetuates the vicious cycle of trauma: from war and poverty to addiction, child abuse, natural disasters, and cultural traumas. I learned that victims unconsciously seek repetition of trauma, and often become history's next aggressors. I was deeply struck by how this concept could shed light and understanding on much of the incomprehensible and tragic violence so prevalent in the world. My body tingled and my mind raced as it occurred to me that cycles of violence could be broken if we understood the roots of our trauma-based behavior, enabling a healing process to follow. It became clear to me that this understanding could be of enormous value worldwide. With my heritage as a driving force, I set out to begin this work in the Middle East.

Traumatic events have shaped many transitions in my life. In May 1947, I was born to Mizrahi Jewish parents in Syria, where my family had its roots for centuries. In December of that year, the U.N. approved the partition of Palestine into two states. The French had recently left Syria, which had been a French protectorate since World War I. Riots against Jews broke out in the streets of Aleppo and Damascus and my family fled overnight to Lebanon. We were among the last Jews allowed to freely leave Syria for the next fifteen years.

I had a happy and peaceful childhood in Lebanon, but civil troubles erupted there in 1958. A bomb hit the building we lived in and we left, once again overnight, the country that had received us so well and where we felt we belonged. We spent a year in Europe while waiting for our immigration papers to Brazil and finally arrived in this exotic foreign culture. In Brazil, I spent my adolescent years in a very tightly knit Jewish-Syrian-Lebanese community and attended French schools. We ate Arabic food; we listened to Arabic music; belly dancers entertained at our weddings; I spoke Portuguese, Arabic, and French interchangeably at home. Years later I immigrated to Israel on a scholarship in art, and left when I met my Canadian husband-to-be. I lived in Canada, became a Canadian citizen, and soon after moved to the United States.

The ongoing and tragic conflict in the Middle East has left me on edge as far back as I can remember, deeply worried about my people and the many family members who lived in Israel. I was torn inside; I couldn't allow myself to hate "the enemy." As Jews, we had lived among the Arabs in fair harmony, and as my father always told us, we could live together very well. I know both cultures well.

Peter Levine's single sentence in 1994, "trauma is at the root of violence," lit a spark under my feet and set me on the path to study trauma and the methods of healing. While I was deeply perturbed by my knowledge about trauma's impact and its incalculable costs to individuals and society, I was also astounded and excited by the recently amassed large reservoir of knowledge for curing trauma. New information coming from both research and the clinical field was transforming the field of trauma healing at an accelerated rate. An explosion of short-term methodologies promised a more rapid resolution. A surge of deep hope emerged. I wondered if this burgeoning of efficient techniques could heal society and move us toward a new age of harmony. I realized that methods of healing trauma could be taught to the public at large and that children could be taught trauma prevention and resiliency. Could this be a way out of the dreadful traumatic legacy of this last century with its unspeakable atrocities, pain, and mass dislocation? Was this a spiritual gift left to us at the threshold of the new century to help us heal humanity and usher in an age of social harmony? The events of September 11 only confirmed my certainty that trauma is one of the most urgent and daunting problems we must solve if humanity is not to slide into a dark age.

I realized that healing could be accomplished with the help of the new theories and techniques, but that private clinical practice was not a large enough response. I specialized in cross-cultural therapy and was treating people from fifty different countries, but the work could not be contained in a therapist's office alone. We could not solve the problems by working only with the privileged few who had enough time and money for therapy. I saw these new techniques as ushering the democratization of healing.

I realized that mass healing requires mass information, and mass information needs mass media. As I researched the role of the media in all its forms—news, entertainment (TV or movies), written media, music lyrics, or video games—it became clear that the media was intrinsically implicated in trauma and violence as it reported on and at times unwittingly amplified it. The media plays a role, but ultimately a reflective one. It supplies what sells. Indeed, the media mirrors society and society mirrors the media. Both the media and the public it informs are caught in the same trauma loop. The roots of rampant violence and senseless destruction in communities and between nations, and their pervasive portrayal in the media, can be found in the recently acquired knowledge about trauma. Though the media is an easy target, neither accusations nor blame are useful. However, the media is extraordinarily positioned to help cope with trauma, and has the power to bring this message of hope to the public at large. The media is the natural ally that can help transform society, turning the horrors of history into healing and peace.

This book explores the role of the media in the healing of trauma as well as the role of trauma in conflicts between nations. It is intended as an invitation to bring conscious awareness to the phenomenon of instantaneous communication and particularly to the issue of trauma and violence in society and in the media. Informed by the discoveries in the trauma field and psychology, my intent is to create new thinking about why and how the media can disseminate information on trauma to help the public and to explore and suggest guidelines on how to present tragic events so they will contribute healthier coping styles.

September 11, 2001, was a day that distinguished the role of the media as unquestionably vital. They responded to the magnitude and immediate relevancy the tragedy had for everyone, and in ways that already had begun to usher in a new approach. Reporters presented both aspects necessary to this coverage—the trauma and the healing. They covered the shock and gruesome devastation as well as New Yorkers' resources of strength, resilience, and the hope and support shown throughout the world. It was the kind of coverage that helps people successfully deal with life's tragedies. Without calling it thus, the media addressed both the "trauma vortex" and the "healing vortex." These concepts, coined by Peter Levine (creator of Somatic Experiencing), will be more fully explored in this book.

Trauma has finally come out of the closet, and America, like so many other nations in the world, faces a deep sense of unpredictability. Understanding the etiology, sources, and manifestations of trauma becomes every day more vital and will allow us to consider the possibilities of intervention before, during, and after traumatic events. People need help facing an uncertain world stripped of illusions of safety. They need education and support to deal with the mental, physical, and behavioral aftereffects of trauma: fear, irritability and anger, depression and anxiety, hyperarousal and somatic complaints, violence and addictions. We cannot prevent certain traumatic events from happening, but we can prevent them from leaving a traumatic impact on their victims.

Thus, I propose that psychological trauma can serve as an organizing principle rather than a destructive one. The framework of trauma allows for compassion and understanding and can facilitate a satisfactory solution. A number of innovative tools are successfully treating and transforming people's lives. Until this information is widely known, no synthesis, no critical mass, and ultimately no shift in public awareness is possible. Only the media can take on the role of educating a public scarred by trauma.

Most importantly, informed by my personal experience, I also propose a shift in the way we view political situations and conflicts such as the Israeli-Palestinian one. In truth, creating peace through cease-fires and pact signing does not resolve the underlying trauma that seethes beneath the diplomacy, where repeated violence is inevitable. With the help of the media, and utilizing the concepts of the healing and trauma vortex, national interests can be better understood and lives can be saved.

This last decade of my life has been totally committed to understanding, learning, and teaching about trauma. I created a major International Trauma Conference in the Middle East in 1999 and co-founded a Trauma Center in Jerusalem. I recently founded the International Trauma-Healing Institute, based in Los Angeles. In February 2001, I met with the Israeli government to discuss the ideas presented in an article I wrote on the Palestinian-Israeli conflict, called "The Trauma Vortex in Action in the Middle East." It became more pressing for me each day to engage the media on the subject of trauma. I see the solution of resolving trauma at individual, community, national, and international levels coming out of a sincere collaborative effort between the media and trauma specialists, where respect and non-judgment prevail.

I was inspired along the way by Frank Okberg's friendly approach to the media. He is the founder of the Dart Center and creator of a program on trauma and journalism. The media are the eyes, ears, and voice of our collective body, and their role and power has only expanded over decades. Through collaboration, we can support their growing responsibility to serve the public by describing available information of the healing component. I invite media members, trauma specialists, and clinicians to engage in a dialogue on this expanding field.

It has been an exhilarating, challenging, and evolving process to go from helping individuals heal and understand how to apply this knowledge to nations and the political process. But none of the benefits from the discoveries on trauma's etiology and healing can take place without the media's understanding and support. This book is about our need of the media's help to change lives, communities, and societies.

1

WHAT EVERYONE SHOULD KNOW ABOUT TRAUMA

In the last century, we have experienced a staggering number of major and extraordinarily traumatic events that have affected 90 percent of the world's population—two World Wars, the Holocaust, genocides in Asia and Africa, labor camps, massive migrations through exile, mass torture, countless internecine wars, acts of terrorism, authoritarian repressions, ethnic cleansing (Serbia, Rwanda, and other places), millions of homicidal acts, as well as repeated waves of natural disasters. Barely two years into the twenty-first century, we have already experienced major traumatic upheavals such as the September 11 attacks in New York and Washington, the Afghani War, and the Intifada II. It promises to be no less traumatic as it threatens a major outbreak of international terrorism and biochemical threat.

Aside from these global traumatic events there are also a number of "daily" events such as car accidents, surgical or medical procedures, major illnesses, and the all-too-common occurrences of spousal abuse, child abuse, as well as assault and rape. All are evidence of our exposure to direct or secondhand trauma at some point in our lives. While most people rebound from trauma on their own, too many remain deeply troubled, leaving a staggering cost to society. This is why it is essential to deal with trauma consciously and knowledgeably and at a mass level.

The truth is that traumatic events are a common reality. The statistics in the U.S. alone are staggering. Twenty-three percent of American adolescents are victims of physical or sexual assaults or witnesses of violence against others. The majority of U.S. psychiatric inpatients and 90 percent of our prison population have histories of severe trauma. Similar numbers hold throughout the industrial world, and numbers in the Third World are devastating. In the U.S., 76 percent of adults report having been exposed to extreme stress, while 15.2 percent of veterans and 1.07 million teenagers currently suffer from trauma.

The gradual but relentless emergence from society's shadow of physical, emotional, and sexual child abuse has brought with it widespread recognition of a more developmental and cumulative form of trauma, even more damaging than shock trauma. Developmental trauma has more to do with the struggle for survival of the spirit and the self than with the integrity of the body.

A proposal for the government called *Child abuse in America: prevalence, costs, consequences and intervention,* by Bessel van der Kolk and his colleagues, as well as other surveys, have yielded surprising information about the costs of trauma: "more than 3 million children are reported for abuse and neglect, each year, [while] the direct cost of abuse is estimated at $22 billion per year."

Doctors in the U.S. say they can find nothing medically wrong with at least 65 percent of patients seeking help. A significant portion of these individuals undoubtedly suffer from symptoms related to trauma and stress. Conservative estimates of the number of children in the United States exposed to a traumatic event in one year exceed three million and the numbers are on the rise. In one U.S. survey of seven- to ten-year-olds, 71 percent said they were afraid of getting shot or stabbed at school or at home, and 63 percent worried they might die young. The statistics on veterans are equally staggering. Ironically, although so many people are traumatized, many do not know they are suffering from trauma, nor do the people around them. The act of naming gives mastery. The formal diagnosis of Post-Traumatic Stress Disorder (PTSD) is a recent and critical first step in making it possible to identify the effects of overwhelming experiences on body and spirit. It has led to an explosion of scientific studies that has engaged us to reexamine many popular prejudices about the effects of trauma. Now we have the proper interventions for people who have too long felt stigmatized, "crazy," or wrongly diagnosed.

In light of new findings through research on the nature of trauma, its costs and manifestations, one of the goals of this book is to give the media a sufficient and effective trauma language to use and incorporate in its reporting.

The media can become a bridge between scientific and clinical research on the one hand and common understanding of trauma on the other by disseminating helpful concepts on the nature of trauma that the public needs to know. Society can make leaps and bounds in gaining mastery over trauma with the media's help. Relaying the following most salient concepts can already benefit the public.

Trauma affects different people in different ways
There are many variables

This concept alone can help alleviate much suffering that comes from judging one's reaction by comparing it to others'. Indeed, what traumatizes one person might not traumatize another. And what is traumatizing at one time for the same person might not be traumatizing at another time; and the reaction to trauma might differ over time for the same person. Understanding this allows us to drop the need to label and judge ourselves, or others, when faced with negative manifestations of trauma, and to look instead for root causes and solutions.

Past relationships and attachments, and the learning derived from them, will affect how people cope with trauma. Even gestation and birth can be traumatizing. (The suffering and traumatization of crack babies is well documented.) Socioeconomic, cultural, and religious contexts can make a person more or less vulnerable to traumatization. Age, personality, and previous traumatic life experiences are also a determining factor. In the same vein, historical, religious, and cultural "old traumas" can make nations more or less vulnerable to the impact of new traumatic situations.

Traumatic events can be ordinary events

Even seemingly small events can be devastating and trigger traumatic symptoms. An attack by an animal (whether a dog, a cat, or a bee) often leaves a person forever frightened of that animal. Several children or an adult pinning down and mercilessly tickling a younger child can leave the child fearful and extremely shy. A group of children playing in the pool pushing the head of one under water for too long and too often leaves this child scared of the water and, even more tragically, can make her fear and mistrust people and withdraw from their company.

A minor car accident, a fall, a high fever in a child, or a medical procedure can be traumatizing. The event might have overwhelmed the person's capacity to cope because of low resiliency, the element of surprise, a previous traumatic experience, genetic or family background, the lack of understanding of their surroundings, and so on.

To infants and young children, even hospitalization can be terrifying and traumatizing. Without appropriate support, a child does not have the inner resources to comprehend the blinding lights, physical restraints, surgical instruments, and drug-induced altered states of consciousness. Nor are they able to sort out their confusion and make sense of waking up alone in a recovery room to the unearthly tones of electronic monitoring equipment and the random coming and going of strangers. In 1946, Dr. David Levy presented scientific evidence that children in hospitals for routine reasons often experience the same "nightmarish" symptoms as "shell-shocked" soldiers. We are just beginning to understand the implications of such findings to society's well being.

Childhood abuse can leave devastating traumatic effects

Child abuse creates PTSD reactions similar to those found in war veterans. Chronic childhood trauma disrupts the child's brain development and imprints long-lasting biological changes. These changes can manifest in the form of depression, chronic anxiety, destructive behavior against self or others, and even suicide. Most abused children do not turn to violence, but some do become teenage delinquents and engage in violent and antisocial behaviors.

The brain develops sequentially, beginning in utero and continuing throughout life. This explains why early trauma has lasting effects. The brain remains sensitive or "plastic" to experience throughout life—but the brainstem and midbrain, which develop first, are less plastic than the cortex. This means that early traumatic experiences registered by the primitive brain can cause long lasting and sometimes permanent damage, negatively influencing the brain's organization and its future functional capabilities. Actual chemical changes occur.

According to Dr. Bessel van der Kolk, professor of psychiatry at HRI Trauma Center, School of Medicine, at the University of Boston and one of the leaders in the field of trauma research, a growing body of research points to potential connections of early trauma with a wide range of learning and adjustment problems among young people. Hyperactivity and Attention Deficit Disorder (ADD) are rampant in schools. Ten to 20 percent of elementary school students in some districts take Ritalin, and rates of adolescent depression and suicide have tripled since World War II. The ability of abused people to maintain emotional balance is severely compromised and their lives often become unmanageable, resulting in high rates of family problems, chronic illness, and suicide.

Any and all types of abuse can produce effects on the psyche and on brain chemistry that may in turn lead to chronic anxiety and depression. Abuse engenders chronic fears, which live on in the victims as if it were continuing at the present moment. Other scenarios, such as a lack of bonding and attachment during early childhood, can also cause emotional scarring that may last into adulthood.

Trauma narrows our choices for survival

When we do not succeed at a survival task, our body/mind predicts we will never succeed at this task and this "knowledge" then informs our subsequent choices in life. After such an experience, options become closed to us. We do not choose reactions to danger according to the current situation, but instead from past conditioning. For instance, Tom, even though he was a burly forty-five-year-old man, felt weak and powerless and allowed other people to take advantage of him. A school assistant, eight years older than him, had raped Tom when he was eleven years old. It was an attack that he could not have escaped and that left him traumatized. At eighteen, a boy a bit smaller than him attacked him sexually. Though he could have escaped, he froze. His reaction as a child of having been overpowered conditioned his reactions to this latest situation.

Trauma is costly to society

There has been much written about the deterioration of the health of the planet. We have failed, however, to address the far-reaching political, social, medical, and psychological deterioration that comes from being exposed to ongoing trauma. Effects of trauma include the physical abuse and neglect of young children, drug abuse, sexual exploitation, and physical and mental illness. In addition to the millions that are seriously traumatized and whose lives are definitely compromised, many others live some of their lives in a state of anxiety, fatigue, depression, burnout, and illness. Nesse and Williams, in their book, *Why Do We Get Sick,* cite a Gallup poll that reported that up to 25 percent of the American workforce suffers from excess stress or anxiety. *USA Today* reported, in the *Report of the National Commission on Sleep Disorders,* that 60 percent of doctor visits are connected to stress and the physical ailments it can cause—which may well include heart disease, high blood pressure, and other auto-immune diseases. The cost to business is $50–75 billion a year, according to Rosch in his *Is Job Stress America's Leading Adult Problem? A Commentary.* No doubt our fast-paced lifestyle and the weakening of family and community support account for much of these problems, but some of them are the result of lingering personal and collective trauma.

People often do not recognize that they suffer from trauma

Too many people are left bewildered by traumatic symptoms they do not recognize as such: panic attacks, unexplained anxiety, phobias and physical pain, mood swings or sleep disturbances, and loss of sexual desire. Too often these symptoms may seem totally unrelated to traumatic events, because they may surface months and even years after the event. Ellen, a woman architect who had a hysterectomy and a car accident in the space of six months, did not realize that the anxiety and depression she was experiencing in her life over a year later were related to these two events, instead blaming tensions in her marital relationship due to her lack of sexual desire. Diana, a lovely thirty-five-year-old woman struggling with a weight gain of thirty pounds, tried one diet after another for two years. She could not understand why she had suddenly put on so much weight, until she started therapy and understood her weight gain was due to being in a car collision four years earlier. She did not know that it could be a symptom of a traumatic response, or that it could manifest so long after the traumatic event.

Traumatic memories are stored differently than other experiences

Traumatic memories can disappear and take years to reappear or manifest as symptoms, according to Dr. Bessel van der Kolk's research. Traumatic memories are indelible and do not change with time as other memories do. They can also be stored at the implicit, unconscious level, embedded in the body, and not be explicitly, consciously remembered. Symptoms may remain dormant for years. Reminders can trigger reactions that have been hidden for years.

Trauma can be crazy-making

Trauma's manifestations are innumerable and are a normal result of the overwhelming impact of too much stress on the nervous system. But the variety of symptoms and the difficulty in relating them to the event that provoked them often make it hard for people to comprehend what's happening to them. A colleague reported that one of her clients complained of terrible stomachaches for a whole year. He did not realize that his pain was related to his experience of living through the San Francisco earthquake, during which he was jolted out of his sleep. For several minutes after he woke up, he did not know whether his wife and two-year-old daughter had survived, resulting in his stomach tightening with a terrible anxiety.

People with unresolved trauma fear they are going crazy! They feel out of control, which makes them easily doubt their sanity. Furthermore, trauma's mysterious manifestations make it difficult for people close to victims of trauma to relate to their symptoms. Well-meaning family and friends often urge trauma victims to "move on" or to "get over it." This only complicates healing, causing victims to become more ashamed of their problems, stop talking about them, ignore them, or avoid treatment. Others become even more ensconced in their victimhood, resenting the lack of validation and fearing being seen as malingerers.

Trauma has remained a secret in the closet of guilt and shame

People too often feel responsible for the trauma that befalls them, which eventually converts to guilt and shame. Trauma makes them feel worthless, diminished, and with poor self-esteem. Trauma stories become secrets buried deep within, and denial or secrecy becomes the victims' defense of last resort. This is especially true for children. Cindy was a saucy and attractive fifty-four-year-old woman whose stepfather sexually abused her when she was four. She held the distorted conviction that it was her fault and hid the abuse for fifty years. Even though, intellectually, she understood that she wasn't responsible for his masturbating in front of her, she could not release her childhood emotions of guilt and shame until she processed the trauma in therapy at the body/mind level.

People with unresolved trauma can also feel shame because they do not react to life in a normal way:

- A door slams and they jump or get easily angry;
- Their reactions to events are different and more negative than others'; they overreact to minor stimuli as they are already hyperactivated; they scream and cry very easily;
- It takes them a long time to settle their nervous system;

- They eat or drink more than others. They have more areas of their lives outside of their control;
- They cannot control their behavior and thus cannot keep their promises;
- They feel "flaky," misunderstood, and often underestimated;
- They have to keep apologizing or avoid people, or people keep their distance from their difficult behavior or hard-to-witness pain.

When people understand that their need for secrecy and their feelings of guilt and shame are part of the trauma experience, they will be better able to let go of the shame and to bring their secrets into the open.

Telling the trauma story in chronological order may be more traumatizing

Trauma has an obsessive quality to it. We need to repeat our traumatic story many times in the attempt to make sense of it. But when we recount it in chronological order, without paying attention or attending to our arousal, it can intensify the trauma and destabilize our nervous system again. We all know of people telling their traumatic stories over and over again and getting more and more upset.

Certain events are more damaging than others

Though they all affect the nervous system, some events debilitate our resources and capacity to hope and trust much more than others. For instance, traumas that result from man's evil are harder to integrate than natural disasters or accidents. An abuse perpetuated by a person we depend on or trust will be more damaging than that of a stranger. Sexual abuse by family members is shattering.

Sexual abuse by a mother, who is the archetypal protector, is even more devastating than by a father or a sibling.

Support and validation, or lack thereof, have an impact on the individual in the aftermath of a traumatic event

Reaching down to get her address book from her purse, in a costly moment of inattention, Anne, a forty-year-old French teacher living in Los Angeles, hit the car ahead of her, whose driver was a plastic surgeon. The glass of her windshield shattered and she suffered from many cuts on her arms and a particularly ugly gash on her face. The plastic surgeon, who had not been hurt, was not only very understanding but ran her to the hospital and later operated on her. Filled with gratitude for his kindness and caring, she not only had no symptoms but also decided to help other victims of accidents by writing a column on trauma.

But Armand had a different experience. He had gotten lost at the beach when he was two years old and was terrified, crying and searching for his mom, when the lifeguard spotted him and helped him find her. When she saw him, she ran to him, slapped him three times strongly, and admonished him to never wander away again. Armand couldn't understand that his mom was reacting because she was terrified and feeling guilty he had disappeared. He interpreted her slaps as her not caring for him and not being concerned by his feelings. At forty-eight, when he described the incident in therapy, he still felt the heat of the slaps on his cheeks, still believed his mother did not care for him, was very insecure with women, and had not been able to secure a lasting relationship.

Only love, understanding, and validation can help a traumatized person come out more intact from trauma. If invalidated, or simply misunderstood or rushed to "get our act together," it becomes almost impossible not to become defensive and to not stay stuck in the trauma. Vietnam veterans present an example of traumatic suffering worsened by returning home to a hostile and rejecting nation. Many of those veterans developed symptoms of PTSD from their war traumas. But having come back to anti-war posters and rejection, they were further traumatized by the post-war hostile reception they received upon their return and by the lack of positive closure. Consider the shocking fact that more Vietnam veterans have died from suicide than soldiers who died in the war. Many others were so shattered by their experiences that they became demoralized, institutionalized, addicted, or homeless.

If we had been able to possess today's awareness and understanding of trauma, and had the veterans been offered access to trauma practitioners trained in the new methods, many of these shattered men and women might be leading more productive lives.

Traumatized people tend to reenact their trauma

Reenactment is an energetic and biochemical phenomenon. It is a concept so important to society that we will cover it in greater detail in Chapters 2 and 4. Often trauma takes on a life of its own, leading individuals to engage in patterns of repetitive reenactment. Their traumatic response may be triggered by new intense stimuli or by conscious or unconscious reminders of earlier traumatic events. The traumatic stress response becomes chronic by lack of discharge or by recurring exposure. It creates the drive for a vicious cycle of reenacting traumatic events and further traumatization.

The "trauma vortex," a metaphor coined by Peter Levine to describe the whirlpool of chaos in the aftermath of trauma, aptly conveys this self-perpetuating, repetitive, out-of-control spiral of energy that keeps amplifying as it swirls downward, generating a crescendo of internal chaos, panic, and fear. The vortex image is similar to patterns found in tornadoes, hurricanes, and whirlpools that suck in what they find on their path. Nature repeats in our bodies. This dynamic image can be a useful model for understanding a wide range of phenomena that beset millions of individuals in contemporary societies, as well as whole nations.

Trauma can shatter families and relationships

Traumatic arousal can precipitate anger and intensity, or withdrawal and numbing of all emotions. Such psychic numbing and/or overreaction make it extremely difficult for family members to fully participate in meaningful interpersonal relationships.

Since traumatized individuals have difficulty maintaining healthy relationships, trauma's destructive effects strike the family system particularly hard. Intimacy and trust are compromised between adults; polarization and intolerance exaggerate the natural differences between people. Traumatized individuals are often less able to experience empathy or to feel they are on the "same side" as their partners. This directly impacts communication, understanding, and cooperation. Too often tragedy breaks up couples rather than uniting them. Spouses, children, and extended family members are also vulnerable to vicarious trauma, thus spreading symptoms throughout the family system.

Parenting requires good judgment, consistency, love, and the provision of security and stability. These essential elements of good parenting are undermined by post-traumatic conflict and confusion. This understanding alone has helped many couples involved in clinical practice stay together, after they were able to identify how many of their problems were trauma generated.

"The body keeps the score"

So says Dr. Bessel van der Kolk in reference to how traumatic experiences can alter brain structure and chemistry, thereby wrecking havoc on the body and mind. Maria Do Carmo's story illustrates trauma's impact on a person's biology. Three hooded men kidnapped Maria, a Brazilian decorator, on her way to a meeting with a client. The kidnappers kept her in the trunk of their car for a whole day before her family was able to negotiate and pay the ransom for her freedom. She was then left on a highway in the middle of the night. There were few cars on the road, and nobody stopped to help her. It took her another four excruciating hours to reach home.

Months after the event, Maria felt she was still living at the edge of insanity. Her normally strong coping mechanisms had been overwhelmed by the suddenness of the event, the impossibility to fight or flee, and the consequent feeling of utter helplessness that washed over her. Feeling generally anxious, she slept poorly and felt disconnected and isolated from everyone. She continually relived the moment she was approached, the moment they gagged her, and the moment they forced her in the trunk. She jumped at minor sounds, felt unprotected unless she was in her house, and could not walk in the city she had always loved without constantly looking behind her. As hard as she tried, she could not gain control of her nervous system. She became very irritable. Maria's nervous system had clearly been affected and her symptoms were getting worse. She was later helped with Somatic Experiencing. After only a few sessions she was able to lessen some of her nervous energy and resolve her fears.

Trauma affects health

Undischarged traumatic energy takes a tremendous toll on our health. "The human body," said Dr. Pamela Peeke of the University of Maryland in *Newsweek* (June 14, 1999), "was never meant to deal with prolonged chronic stress. We weren't meant to drag around bad memories, anxieties and frustrations." In the 1980s, researchers at the National Institutes of Health found that an important precursor for the development of heart disease was "emotional toxicity," or our emotional reactions to the events in our lives. There is a growing body of medical literature indicating that patients with unexplained physical symptoms, ranging from intestinal tract problems to various forms of heart disease, may have a history of physical, sexual, or shock trauma.

A research study of 16,000 people by the Center for Disease Control in Atlanta showed that adults who were abused as children are vastly more likely to become smokers, alcoholics, and drug abusers or to suffer from obesity. The immune system is also affected. Victims of abuse have significantly higher rates of lung disease, diabetes, heart disease, and cancer. More specific studies have shown that women with histories of chronic sexual abuse were more prone to disorders of the immune system.

Trauma can lead to substance abuse and addictive behaviors

Drugs and alcohol are often the self-medications of choice for dealing with the emotional turmoil of trauma. Drug abuse places a burden on the whole of society. While the actual annual costs are unknown, they have been estimated at some $60 billion, including lost productivity by drug users, the costs of drug-related crime, and welfare and health care services. How much of this is trauma related?

It is noteworthy that the media has taken a leadership role in promoting awareness, education, and healing in the area of substance abuse.

Trauma can jeopardize mental health

People who carry unresolved psychological trauma may turn their emotions against themselves, resulting in anxiety, depression, anger, or self-destructive behaviors, including suicide. People who have been traumatized commonly believe:

- The world is an unfriendly place; it is unpredictable or immoral;
- There is no justice or fairness in the world;
- Life is always disappointing; things can't work out;
- People are dangerous or cannot be trusted;
- Something will always go wrong;
- They are not in control of their destiny or cannot protect themselves.

Guilty and ashamed, traumatized individuals can feel as if something is deeply wrong with their core self.

Trauma can haunt you all your life

The impact of trauma can be pervasive and destructive to the lives of individuals, families, and communities long after the actual events have passed. In addition, cultural and religious traumas have impacted the history of many nations through wars and displacements, often decades later.

Trauma can lead to aggression

Aggression against others has been particularly well documented in war veterans, traumatized children, and prisoners with histories of early trauma. Studies have shown that 90 percent of most violent criminals in prisons have a history of child abuse. Violence is too often the effect of traumatic anger directed outward into the world, manifesting people's incapacity to manage and control their stuck arousal. Connection to both the self and to others is interrupted by trauma, thus facilitating indifference toward the well being of others. According to the *Journal of the American Medical Association*, deaths and injuries inflicted by firearms cost the United States about $20 billion every year in hospitalizations and other medical costs.

At the international level, we are seeing children orphaned by war, raised in a climate of terror and strife, become easy prey to leaders with rigid polarized belief systems, and comprise a next generation of terrorists or armies on the rampage. In some countries these groups have turned their aggression, mistrust, and paranoia toward their women, the very gender they needed as children but were not able to be raised or nurtured by. For example, many of the Taliban are orphans brought up away from mothers and women in general.

Trauma leads to paranoid, self-defeating, and polarized belief systems

Unresolved trauma can affect whole populations. Traumatic reactions such as paranoia and polarized thinking resulting in demonization and dehumanization of the other may be the rationale behind reenactment of trauma at the level of nations. This concept is further elaborated in Chapter 2.

Trauma as a root cause of violence must be understood in order to help stem the violence

Understanding and exploring the concept of trauma and the frustration of needs as the underlying cause for one's own violence, or the violence of others, allows a better grasp of the problem and may offer ways to get out of the victim/perpetrator loop.

Basic needs are frustrated in trauma

As Ervin Staub showed in his book, *The Roots of Evil,* trauma makes people fulfill needs in a destructive way. As it creates a narrow focus of attention and makes people lose their ability to reason and "weigh consequences," trauma impels people to attempt to satisfy some of their needs at the expense of their other legitimate needs. And obviously, it impels to totally disregard the needs of the "other."

It is easier for traumatized people to give up their judgment and individuality and believe they are joining a bigger cause

They may believe they can escape their own pain by joining an ideology or a movement that reflects their unsatisfied needs, no matter how destructive these movements are. It allows them to not get in touch with the devastation of the losses suffered and thus feel better by connecting and surrendering to the power of the group.

Power and violence are seen as a means to recuperate a sense of control and effectiveness

Trauma's greatest impact is the sense of total helplessness and loss of control, while the need to feel in control of one's life is one of people's most basic needs.

Trauma is contagious

The impact of trauma often manifests in panic and despair and/or aggressive and violent responses. These powerful feelings are contagious. Families, clans, tribes, and nations are particularly affected by the contagiousness of their members' trauma.

> The trauma of a critical mass of individuals in a society can suddenly transform into collective trauma, with a tremendous impact on the actions of that collective.

The sea of irrationality and murderous madness that can sweep a society forever stuns us; we are forever unable to comprehend how normal people can get caught in it. It is crucial for the international community, governments, and nations to understand what a traumatic response looks like. It is crucial that we learn to help those responses run their energy through without getting caught in it. It is crucial to break the impulse to use traumatic responses to attack the other. It is also important to understand that the aggressive trauma vortex of one group or nation may well engage a traumatic vortex response from the party aggressed. Only by recognizing our traumatic reactions and the traumatic reactions of "the others," can we help to orient each other and contain these reactions. Otherwise, this energy goes into secondary and tertiary loops and people become more and more diminished in their capacity to keep control over their emotions of fear and panic and the consequent aggression.

Trauma makes victims participate in their own victimization

Seeking justice in the form of revenge and violence simply makes people participate in their further traumatization. Groups and nations can fall into the "no one cares about us," "we don't count," and "we are always forgotten, abandoned, disrespected, and dismissed" mentalities, seeking solace, justice, and revenge in violence and forgetting all the efforts and groups that have worked together in the past for togetherness—all the ones who cared and helped. We all need to remember—the parties involved as well as the spectators—that the pull of the trauma vortex is stronger and easier to follow than to resist. Here the media can play a crucial role, first by not falling into the contagiousness themselves, then by recognizing historically "inherited trauma." They can validate all the parties' traumatization and wounds without indulging in their victimization or in giving them the underdog role, and help them move through the trauma vortex by indicating, exploring, and uncovering other means of resolving the conflict.

This chapter introduced some of the invisible costs of trauma that are never calculated. The costs to families, business, social services, as well as to peace between nations are staggering. And they will remain uncalculated until the media educates the public, government, and business about the magnitude of trauma. This could have interesting implications for domestic priorities and budget discussions, as well as for international politics.

The vast majority of human beings show an astounding resiliency in the face of tragedy. They go on to rebuild their lives, their relationships, their homes, and their countries. Tragedy tests character, and through it many individuals, communities, and nations discover enormous reservoirs of strength, courage, and magnanimity. Often its challenge brings new meaning, and leads to more fulfilling spiritual paths.

However, even people who are able to overcome tragedy and lead productive lives may still be more easily overwhelmed by later stressful events or have a part of their life affected by the residual unresolved energy. Society cannot afford to keep paying this tremendous price for untreated trauma. Most importantly, trauma is preventable, treatable, and curable.

2

THE "TRAUMA VORTEX" AND THE "HEALING VORTEX"

According to Peter Levine, "Trauma has been perhaps the most avoided, ignored, belittled, denied, misunderstood, and untreated cause of human suffering."

Until very recently, it was believed to create irreparable damage.

WHAT IS TRAUMA?

I am using a very broad definition of trauma as the emotional, biological, and psychological impact suffered in response to an actual or perceived threat to one's life, body, and identity and that stays stuck in the system. It is any occurrence in the past, which, when we recall it, could bring up all or some of the following:

- Difficult emotions and perturbing and overwhelming physical symptoms;
- Negative and destructive beliefs, images, desires, and fantasies;
- Compulsions, obsessions, and addictions;
- Dissociation (the ability to step out of one's body in order to avoid scary feelings);
- Blocked development, a fractured sense of self and

wholeness, and a hindered centeredness and spiritual connection.

A traumatic event is a threatening event that overwhelms our capacity to respond to it physiologically, mentally, and psychologically. It may break our defenses—our body's stimulus barrier—so suddenly and with such brutal force that we cannot react to it effectively. It creates memory at the cellular level, often manifesting as persistent painful bodily sensations. It may leave us feeling overwhelmingly helpless, intensely fearful, fragmented, and stuck. We may feel drained, depressed, hurt, guilty, or ashamed, without control and without access to our resources. Our emotional reactions can be unwarranted, irrational, and exaggerated. Our choices to live an intentional life in alignment with our potential are reduced.

Trauma is made of the traumatizing event and the subjective meaning we give to it. The interpretation of meaning can continue to evolve long after the event has passed. Dr. Bessel van der Kolk once gave the example of a woman who did not develop PTSD at the time she was raped, but rather a year later when she discovered her attacker not only raped but also killed another woman. The realization that she too could have been killed created the PTSD. Paradoxically, this process of evolving meaning over time can also be used in the healing of trauma. This is where the media, I believe, is uniquely positioned to play an important leadership role, as I will elaborate later.

In recent years, research has shown that Post-Traumatic Stress Disorder is one of our most common psychiatric problems. People who develop PTSD become "stuck" in the trauma and are under the grip of continuous fear or anxiety. Safety in the world and relaxation in the body are no longer attainable. Their self-image becomes distorted and their ways of dealing with future stress are profoundly affected. As van der Kolk explains in his *Approaches to the Treatment of PTSD*, "Terrifying experiences that rupture people's sense of predictability and invulnerability can profoundly alter the ways that they subsequently deal with their emotions and their environment." However, when I talk about trauma in this book, I am addressing not only PTSD, but also much milder forms of traumatization. While 10 to 20 percent of people who are exposed to traumatic events may develop serious PTSD, many more people remain highly functioning, but have some areas in their lives impacted by trauma.

The Dynamics of the Trauma Vortex

The trauma vortex is a metaphor that describes the whirlpool of chaos in trauma's aftermath. Also called the "black hole" of trauma by van der Kolk, it is a downward spiral that traps the traumatized. Peter Levine, author of *Waking the Tiger: Healing Trauma*, coined this term to describe this self-perpetuating downward spiral of traumatic images and memories, sensations and feelings. Individuals trapped in the trauma vortex become unable to control their sensations, images, feelings, thoughts, and behaviors.

Traumatic events leave individuals (and nations) shaken to their core. As early as 1889, Pierre Janet, the foremost nineteenth-century French trauma specialist, had already observed that traumatized patients reacted to reminders of the trauma with emergency responses that had been relevant to the original trauma but had no bearing on current experience. But this information had not penetrated the public's consciousness, and only recently are people learning that this irrationality is neither mysterious nor genetically based.

Trauma occurs when a person is overwhelmed by a harrowing and distressing event that his nervous system is unable to assimilate, when the arousal is too great and too rapid to digest. Even a single experience can alter a person's psychological, biological, and social balance. The memory of one particular event can taint many others. Instinctive survival mechanisms summon powerful energies to meet the threat. In trauma, these energies are not completely discharged and remain fixed in the nervous system. This excess energy throws the system off balance and symptoms may manifest within a widespread continuum, in myriad ways, in one or more of the following manners:

- People affected by trauma cannot stop revisiting the horrible images of the event. Unable to control their intrusive thoughts, they ruminate obsessively, repeatedly asking themselves the same questions: "Why me? What if. . .? How can I change what happened? What's wrong with me?" They cannot control feelings of fear and terror, even though the event is over.

- They are overcome by a sense of utter despair and hopelessness. Everything seems meaningless. Life's normal sense of security and ease seem to be gone forever. Nothing seems trustworthy anymore.

- Deep feelings of inadequacy, shame, guilt, and hurt pride come in waves. Especially when they are the victims of man-made traumas, people have a profound feeling of being out of grace, feeling abandoned by God, by others, and by life. Their fundamental needs for safety, for the right to exist without danger and to trust the good will of others, and their sense of empowerment are shaken. The sense of predictability, competency, and the ability to control one's destiny are gone.

- The strength of these chaotic feelings, sensations, and thoughts leaves them bewildered and questioning their sanity. They cannot use reason. They lose their capacity to see events and situations in a balanced, composed way. Everything can feel extreme and off.

- Reminders of the event, such as aftershocks from earthquakes or the sounds of sirens, can trigger upsetting memories of their initial pain, helplessness, and suffering. Individuals may become hypersensitive to sound, smell, or touch. All the senses can be affected. These "triggers" may be accompanied by fears that the stressful event will be repeated.

- People might have vivid and repeated images or memories of the event. Flashbacks may seem to occur for no apparent reason and may lead to physical reactions such as rapid heartbeat and sweating. Thoughts and behavior patterns are also affected.

- People may experience confusion, obsessive and negative thinking, and difficulty concentrating.

- People different from them that they could previously tolerate suddenly appear threatening and dangerous. The natural tendency to differentiate between themselves and others becomes polarized, and their thoughts and emotions about the "other" become obsessive.

- Anger and rage mount, coupled with a deep sense of powerlessness at their ability to right the situation. It is a rage that can be turned against themselves and/or against others.

- The effects of trauma can manifest rapidly or have a long gestation period. They are manifold and can be devastating. At the individual level, traumatic symptoms manifest as psychosomatic problems.
  - Physically: chronic pains, hyperarousal, flashbacks, and nightmares.

- • Emotionally: feelings of terror, rage and helplessness, depression, numbness, and confusion.

- • Mentally: paranoid beliefs, blame, judgment, criticism, and polarized thinking.

- • Behaviorally: family disputes, breakups, divorces, impulsive behavior, addictions, family violence, more risky behavior, rise in car accidents.

- Feelings become intense and are sometimes unpredictable. Recurring strong emotional reactions are common. People may be more irritable than usual, subject to dramatic mood swings. They can go through fear and terror, to anger and rage, to resignation and acceptance.

- Interpersonal relationships often become strained. Greater conflict such as more frequent arguments with family members and co-workers is common; or people might withdraw, isolate, or avoid their usual activities.

- Physical symptoms may accompany the extreme stress. Headaches, nausea, and chest pain may result and may require medical attention. Preexisting medical conditions may worsen due to the stress. Basic physiological processes such as sleeping and eating patterns become disrupted.

- At the collective level, whether between groups or nations, we see not only the above symptoms assailing individuals and their families, but also polarized thinking between different groups blaming, stereotyping, scapegoating, demonizing, and dehumanizing the other; identifying the need to destroy "the other" in order to "fulfill the ideology." Seeking justice through violence and revenge appears logically to be the only choice.

Three months after the tragic events of September 11, we saw many signs of the trauma vortex in action: personnel productivity dropping off, a 25 percent increase in the sale of anti-anxiety drugs and sleeping pills, and 20 percent increase in the use of anti-depressants. Six months later, we saw many couples with strained relationships separating, dissatisfied spouses having affairs, more family discord, people feeling numb and indecisive in their work or in their personal lives, and people with paranoid thoughts. We have seen much somatization of stress, with chronic pain problems and other neuro-muscular problems (e.g., neck, back, or joints) on the increase.

The Contagion of Trauma

The trauma vortex is contagious and its pull magnetic. It occupies all of our attention and energies. When traumatized, nothing else matters. Our focus becomes narrowed. We ruminate only on our traumatic narrative, which becomes increasingly distorted over time as more elements of our lives become subjugated to it and contaminated by the original event. In fact, this traumatic narrative encourages and maintains our traumatic state. Victimhood becomes an identity. It may give us a sense of righteousness, a deep relief in thinking we are good and right and that we have been greatly wronged. But it also implies powerlessness, lack of control over our lives, and worst of all, it participates in furthering our victimization.

Our responses, now informed only by trauma, create more trauma in our lives. As we approach life with trepidation, hypervigilance, and mistrust, we generate in turn distrust and suspicion around us, only "confirming" our initial feelings. Moreover, the media may unconsciously amplify our trauma vortex since it reflects what's going on and what we are feeling about it. Thus the media can itself become caught in the same trauma vortex merely by reflecting it. Moreover, traumatic reactions can be re-triggered on anniversary dates by similar stimuli or even predictions of such events.

Predictors of Trauma

Of course, we are all subject to stressors in our lives. However, when the stressful situation is over, normal stress is relieved. With trauma, when the traumatic event is over, the traumatic stress stays. Trauma is when time doesn't heal. Traumatic grief is like traumatic stress. Normal grief takes its course. Traumatic grief is grief mixed with guilt and shame and does not evolve into stages. It stays stuck. There are several predictors for developing traumatic reactions:

- *The magnitude of exposure*: The more intense, lengthy, or shattering the event, the greater the impact and the more difficult the recovery.

- *The age at the time of trauma*: The earlier it is, the more damaging its effect.

- *The experience of prior trauma*: Unresolved prior trauma leaves us more vulnerable to later trauma. Well-processed previous trauma leaves us better prepared and more resilient in the face of future trauma.

- *The environmental conditions existing at the time of the trauma*: Severe poverty, previous conflict within the family or the group, or sudden or rapid changes—psychological, social, political, or technological—can significantly affect the response to traumatic events.

- *The quality of social support during and after the event:* This influences the event's impact. A negative reaction to the suffering from a traumatic event can leave us more traumatized than the event itself.

- *The amount of dissociation during the traumatic event:* The more we dissociate or leave our body, the more vulnerable we are to developing traumatic reactions.

Trauma and the Triune Brain

Over the last few years, research has revealed that trauma is not only an event and the memory of it, but also an event in the body. It is both a neuro-chemical happening in our brain and our response to the external events, our relationship to them. "It is not what happened to you that is significant, but how you make sense of what happened to you," (at the body/mind level), according to Dr. Daniel Siegel, author of *The Developing Mind* and associate clinical professor of psychiatry at the UCLA School of Medicine. Specialists see trauma as a normal, protective survival response gone awry. They define trauma as thwarted instincts—as an incomplete response, a mobilized survival energy that stays un-discharged and trapped in the body.

Trauma alters a number of fundamental brain mechanisms that affect coping behavior, learning, and memory through anatomical changes, altered metabolism, and blood flow. The body's natural system of defense breaks down, causing the autonomic nervous system to disorganize. The altered brain chemistry resulting from trauma not only creates real havoc in people's current lives but also makes them more vulnerable to such events in the future.

The human brain, also called the triune brain, consists of three systems that work together in an integrated way:

- *The reptilian or instinctual brain:* This area is in charge of all the involuntary functions: sleeping, appetite, breathing, temperature regulation, perspiration, sexual function, reproduction, and survival. We can see how trauma can create havoc in the most basic life functions.

- *The limbic, mammalian, or emotional brain:* This brain region is responsible for feelings and emotions and is especially adapted for handling human interactions, which consist of inextricably intertwined emotional and logical signals. It is the center of processing social information, autobiographical consciousness, and evaluation of meaning, activation of arousal, and the coordination of body response in higher cognitive processing.

- *The neo-cortex or thinking brain:* This brain level makes us uniquely human, develops last, and its optimal development depends on the healthy development of earlier systems. It is our thinking brain, our creative system, and what makes us "us." This is where the conscious mind is mediated.

The processing of most sensory input occurs outside conscious awareness. Only novel, significant, or threatening information is passed on to the neo-cortex for further attention by the amygdala, located in the limbic brain. The amygdala sorts out our experiences to identify threat, based on our earlier experiences. If the amygdala signals danger, the stress response is triggered, chemicals surge, and energy builds, milliseconds before the cortex evaluates. If the cortex then decides there's no life-threatening danger, it sends signals to shut down the stress response. We have all experienced this when a loud noise or a siren sends a surge of alarm up the spine, even when we "know" no threat is present; and then we go back to a state of alert relaxation.

But if the threat is assessed as real, the reptilian brain, which is expert on survival, takes over and controls the instinctive response of fight, flight, or freeze. Under its command, the body reacts with a cascade of neuro-hormonal changes, known as the "fight-or-flight" response. Adrenaline is responsible for increases in respiration, heart rate, and blood pressure. The brain releases natural painkillers such as endorphins. Cortisol releases glucose into the bloodstream for quick energy. As a result of this rapid deployment, we have more oxygen available, we push more blood to the brain and muscles, and we are instantly more alert and ready to flee or fight. We flee as a first option. If we cannot and there is the possibility to win, we fight.

Though each of these brain regions has its own specialized function, they act in an integrated way. In trauma, this integrative function is broken and the system is deregulated.

STUCK IN A DEEP FREEZE

The reptilian brain controls the autonomic nervous system, which plays a crucial part in enabling survival. It has traditionally been known as having two branches, the sympathetic and the parasympathetic.

The sympathetic branch of the nervous system is responsible for charging the system, releasing the energy we require to meet our needs for mobility and mobilization. It also shifts resources to muscular, visceral, and other systems as needed to respond to survival functions. Once the threat is passed, the parasympathetic branch takes over and reestablishes homeostasis. It is responsible for rest and rebuild, but also for the immobility response to threat. Under normal conditions, there is a gentle rhythm between the charge of the sympathetic and the discharge of the parasympathetic and life feels good and controllable. With trauma, this rhythm changes drastically.

When faced with what is perceived as inescapable or overwhelming threat, humans and animals use the "freeze" or immobility response. The traumatized person is flooded with fear, terror, rage, and helplessness. In response to these powerful emotions, she protects herself by freezing. She gets, as we say, "frozen with fear," or "scared stiff." This adaptive response provokes an altered state of consciousness shared by all mammals in which no pain is experienced. The physiological mechanism governing this response is not under our conscious control.

The freeze response is implicated in the development of trauma in humans. When animals in the wild come out of this frozen state, they physically discharge the arousal energy through subtle or gross motor activity—trembling, shaking, deep breathing—and then quickly regain full control of their bodies, returning to normal life as if nothing had happened. Problems arise for us humans, however, because we are often unable to come out of the freeze. Instead, we unconsciously override these primitive impulses to shake, afraid of the loss of control attached to the autonomic and involuntary discharge process.

We further add cultural inhibitions of discharge by judging our trembling or shaking bodies as awkward or a sign of weakness. Often, afraid of the powerful feelings of fear and rage that naturally emerge when we get out of the freeze, we revert involuntarily to the freeze reaction when the energy starts to thaw. It is because we override the process of discharge that our nervous system remains aroused and our body and mind respond as if the threat still exists.

The un-discharged freeze response leaves the nervous system deregulated and confused: the sympathetic and the parasympathetic branches no longer participate in a gentle dance of charge and discharge, but step on each other's toes. The sympathetic, fully mobilized, continues to unleash tremendous survival energy while the parasympathetic, geared to control the mobilization of energy, puts the brakes fully on. The person stuck in the freeze response alternates hopelessly between these two opposing forces: symptoms of mobilized energy manifesting as racing heart and pulse, and panic, and symptoms of shut down manifesting as lethargy, fatigue, or disconnection—an extremely tiring and debilitating process.

Moreover, people often feel shame and guilt for having frozen in the face of threat. These two emotions are most responsible for hiding or denying the existence of trauma in our lives. Understanding that the freeze response is instinctual, involuntary, and adaptive can often help individuals who froze in face of threat get over those feelings.

Flooding, feeling physiologically overwhelmed, and freezing—two different but equally painful cycles that haunt traumatized individuals—also have a psychological component. Symptoms of dissociation, numbing, apathy, or depression alternate with the more prevalent symptoms of hyperarousal, anxiety, mania, and angry outbursts. Triggers associated with the traumatizing event will "wake up" the trauma and the intense feelings make the person freeze again. The effect of this is fixed, patterned, and stuck behavior.

Indeed, the tendency of traumatized organisms to revert to irrelevant emergency behaviors in response to minor stress has been well documented in animals in laboratories. Frightened animals tend to avoid novelty, and instead persevere in familiar behavior regardless of the outcome or reward. This is also true for humans.

Regardless of whether the traumatizing threats result from a shock, a single overwhelming event, a seemingly insignificant one, or from an entire history of child abuse—physical and emotional—or neglect, the effect on the nervous system is the same. The body/mind has been mobilized and the energy it produced needs to be discharged. Early traumas may leave more enduring scars, and shock and developmental trauma often overlap with each other.

THE CONSEQUENCES

Consider Stacy's situation: a man in a red shirt brutally assaulted her, held a knife to her throat, scarred her face, and raped her—but she had dissociated from her experience. One day she walks by a store with a red dress in the window; she feels her heart racing; a deep anxiety and a strong urge to run take her over. She doesn't understand why but later she starts avoiding that street, then avoiding that neighborhood, and eventually she stops going out altogether. She came to therapy for agoraphobia and had no insight into the origin of her problem.

Under ordinary conditions, many severely traumatized people, including natural disaster victims, rape victims, battered women, and abused children, still have a fairly good psychosocial adjustment. Signs of their trauma might never show up; however, their future ability to respond to intense stress may be compromised. They may become unable to discriminate a minor stress from a major stressful event. They may overreact to lesser provocations with extreme fear or terror and feel the need to fight or flee when it is not necessary. They respond to a stimulus in a knee-jerk fashion, without making the necessary mental or psychological assessment of what is going on. Their response can be aggravated by a number of circumstances—being under pressure, under the influence of drugs and alcohol, during dream states, in response to the aging process, or on exposure to strong reminders of a traumatic past event.

As the trauma vortex pulls all traumatic associations to it and saps current life of its significance, victims of trauma continue feeling frozen and imprisoned unless they become aware that they have alternative, proactive ways of responding. Traumatized people are not suffering from a disease in the normal sense of the word. They have simply become fixated in an aroused state, in which it is difficult to function normally.

In an image borrowed from Somatic Experiencing, we can imagine our emotional life as a running river with well-secured banks. Upsetting things happen; there are frustrations and ups and downs in everyday life, with some moments more difficult than others. But overall, we feel we are in charge of our emotions. When a traumatic event overwhelms us, there is a breach in the banks of our river of life. We do not feel in control of our emotions, our thoughts, our sensations, nor often of our behavior.

All the elements involved with the trauma are outside of our ability to cope and be in control. This is the formation of the trauma vortex, spiraling off from the flow of one's life, taking on a life of its own, where everything in the environment can become a trigger by association. We start avoiding so many behaviors, places, people, foods, smells, and sounds because they are unconscious reminders of traumatic stimuli previously lived and either forgotten or left unresolved in the nervous system. The nervous system retains memories of what we lived that often our consciousness does not retain.

Indeed, trauma reduces its victims' vitality. It limits their vision and narrows their view of what's possible in their jobs, their relationships, and their social life. To all the threats in the outside world are added the internal threats coming from their traumatized minds or their deregulated nervous systems.

Cheryl, a strong and athletic woman, came to therapy because she could not exercise anymore. She loved to run but had to quit because after a few minutes of running, she would feel overcome by a tremendous anxiety. Eventually, she realized that it was related to an attack at gunpoint she had suffered. Whenever her heart rate reached the same level it had reached when the assailant had held a gun to her forehead, she would feel the same wild heartbeat, which she now read as a sensation of fear. Through the fast heartbeat, her body remembered the big fright she had felt even though she had been able to escape and didn't think she had been affected by the event.

Victims of trauma are obsessed with memories of the past and fears for the future. Danger, for them, in one form or another seems constant. They are prone to repetitive reliving of images, feelings, and physiological states; and to the reenactment of behaviors and interpersonal relationships patterns, all reminiscent of the initial experience.

Furthermore, a new event can trigger long-hidden memories of previous traumas. For example, a sexual assault in adulthood can provoke forgotten memories of childhood sexual abuse.

THE "HEALING VORTEX"
THE INNATE CAPACITY TO HEAL

Although the trauma vortex can be devastating, there is cause for hope. As the intense research conducted during the Decade of the Brain has shown, the brain is plastic and resilient, capable of being profoundly shaped by relationships and experiences throughout the life span. So while it is true that trauma can affect us at any time, it can also be cured at any time. As Dr. Peter Levine, clinical psychologist and founder of the Human Enrichment Foundation asserts in *Waking the Tiger: Healing Trauma*, "My firsthand experience with over 1,000 traumatized people has convinced me that the biochemical or molecular changes are secondary effects—that PTSD is not only preventable, but in many cases its effects are reversible."

The "healing vortex" refers to mankind's innate resiliency, the capacity of people to cope with tragedy and to heal on their own. It is a deeply innate mechanism that brings us back to equilibrium from the brink of terror and insanity. Human beings can rebound from extreme experiences of threat given appropriate guidance, to reconnect with the innate ability to heal when the body gets sick. "People can get from feeling very debilitated and dysfunctional to not only get rid of their symptoms, but really come alive," says Peter Levine. Techniques are available to help the body discharge the traumatic energy and to reverse the downward spiral of the trauma vortex. To accomplish the positive effects of the healing vortex, we need awareness, intention, and action.

The capacity to heal is always present and accounts for humanity's remarkable resiliency. We can reduce our individual and societal traumatic legacies by transforming them. Once they engage in the healing vortex and process their trauma, individuals are often thankful for whatever traumatic event may have happened to them. They are grateful for the richness of the emotional, personal, and spiritual life that is the product of healed trauma.

Bruce Perry, professor of child psychiatry at Baylor University, School of Medicine, and author of *Maltreated Children: Experience, Brain Development and the Next Generation*, points out that human beings evolved through community. This is a critical piece of information. The biology of the brain is designed to keeping small, naked, weak, individual humans alive by being part of a larger biological whole—the family, the clan. We survived and evolved interdependently with one another—socially, emotionally, biologically. The participation of one's community is fundamental to the healing of trauma.

Immediately after the September 11 attacks, we witnessed many signs of the healing vortex in action: Thousands stood in long lines and even put their names on waiting lists to donate blood, after a call went out for blood donations in New York. In the months following the attack, the number of life insurance policies increased, expressing the fear people were feeling, but also their concerns for their families. Many people reflected on their own values and what was important to them, turning toward their families and healing tense relationships. Many people undertook charitable work while others curtailed their appetite for material goods.

New Yorkers astounded us as well as themselves with their deep well of compassion and resources after the September 11 attack. And the media chose to broadcast this very wonderful humane side of mankind so that the rest of us could share in the feelings of community.

Though the last century has known extraordinary catastrophes, the strength of the human spirit has consistently triumphed. Millions of displaced and exiled people have relocated, adopted new cultures, and created viable lives for themselves and their children. Prisoners freed from the hells of the Holocaust and labor camps have started new lives and even established new countries. We saw the generosity of the world community when the collapsed countries of World War II, both victorious and defeated, were helped to rebuild and rise again. Though the last hundred years contained tragic events, they have also been marked by enormous economic and technological success, as well as meaningful progress toward peace between nations.

3

THE TRAUMA VORTEX
AS A ROOT CAUSE OF VIOLENCE
IN INTERNATIONAL CONFLICTS

Researchers have established that the most serious repercussion of unresolved trauma is violence. Trauma begets violence, which begets more trauma, which begets more violence.

When a critical mass in a population has been traumatized, the general population is impacted. The most dangerous aspect of the trauma vortex is the loss of all reasoning power and the hijacking of one's emotions by the amygdala.

Like any individual, any nation can be vulnerable to the irrationality of the trauma vortex.

National signs of the trauma vortex in action can include:

- Aggressive and bellicose language regarding other groups or nations;
- Instilling hatred in children;
- The use of visual or written media to incite polarized thinking;
- Demonizing of "the other";
- Incitement to violence;

- An almost mystical elevation of one's own group, ethnicity, race, religion, or nationality;
- Purge of all foreign entertainment, encouraging xenophobia;
- Severe penalties against independent media and against the discordant intelligentsia;
- Use of state-controlled media to openly encourage killing, genocide, and war.

In summary, all efforts serve the purposes of hatred and war. How might we benefit from better understanding the dynamics of trauma? How can we, as individuals and a society, better deal with traumatic events taking place almost daily? How do conflicts between nations arise and what makes them erupt? Finding answers to these questions, although an always pressing question, has become a critical one as the Middle East trauma vortex is in full swing and as national trauma has burst on the American scene with the events of September 11 that threaten to engulf the whole world.

Unhealed trauma compels one to reenact the ordeal and to polarize, creating an ever-expanding cycle of trauma and violence. We are just beginning to recognize how much collective national traumas may underlie most international conflicts. Knowledge of trauma's impact must inform our analysis of how warring nations act toward each other. This knowledge must inform the interventions of the international community.

Once we recognize the dynamics of trauma and violence, we may be able to slow that process. We may be able to help nations identify when they are under the influence of the trauma vortex. We may be able to warn them and even pressure them, if need be, as soon as we notice the first signs of the trauma vortex.

THE MIDDLE E̶ ̶'T CONFLICT

My vision is that if traum̶ ̶n be resolved and healed on both sides, my father's word could becom̶e̶ ̶ophetic.

I use the Middle East con̶ ̶ct to illustrate the application of the trauma vortex and instinctive survival mechanisms at the political level. Many other trauma vortexes are taking place right this moment, but the Israeli-Palestinian conflict is the one I know best.

The situation in the Middle East seems hopeless. Every day, the media reports stories of trauma and violence and seemingly irreconcilable political positions and narratives agitated by individual and national passions. We become intimately acquainted with accounts of enormous suffering on both sides that leave us ever more resigned and helpless at the incomprehensibility and futility of the situation. The cycle of violence is contagious and spinning out of control. But in reality, *trauma* is contagious. It manifests in violence, which begets more trauma, which begets further violence.

How can the perspective of healthy survival instincts and the use of the trauma vortex concept help us more deeply understand some of the conflicts raging in the world, particularly the daunting Israeli-Palestinian one? To get an idea, we can look at certain events through the lenses of healthy instinctive responses whose results were misunderstood on a global level.

The Withdrawal from Lebanon

The last Israeli soldiers who remained in Lebanon in the first months of the year 2000 were afraid of losing their lives in vain and wanted to go home. They were portrayed as cowards by some writers in the Israeli media, and as having lost their will to fight in the Arab media. However, we need to understand that they were merely in touch with their healthy survival instincts. As long as they believed they were defending the security of their country, they did not protest and dutifully served, although soldiers' lives were lost weekly. Eventually, the country, and especially the soldiers' mothers, recognized the borders were not defensible without exacting a heavy price on both sides, and the public pressured the government for a quicker withdrawal than previously planned. Once it became clear that the Israeli government intended to depart from Lebanon, the soldiers were no longer defending their country but merely sitting ducks before an ever-emboldened enemy.

No one wanted to be among the last to die in meaningless skirmishes. The soldiers had not lost their will to defend themselves. They were rather asserting their instincts to survive. The inaccurate reading of their motivations for leaving Lebanon—as having lost the will to fight—has cost too many lives on both sides and the shattering of the peace process. A more accurate understanding might have dampened attacks by Hezbollah, whose leaders believed the Israelis had departed out of fear. More seriously, Israelis believe the misreading of the situation emboldened Arab attackers in the West Bank to double their efforts, mistakenly believing that if they imitated Hezbollah, Israel would, under the pressure of violence, pull out of the territories as well.

The 1967 Conflict

Another example of the danger of not understanding survival reflexes and trauma took place in 1967, when the Israelis, with the Arab armies threatening them on their borders, initiated a preemptive strike against the Egyptian, Syrian, and Jordanian armies and won the Six Day War. One image the media accentuated was that of thousands of soldiers' boots left in the sand, mistakenly symbolizing the Egyptian army in "cowardly" retreat in the face of an "invincible" Israeli army. However, if we look at this event in terms of healthy fight-flight survival instincts, this was not "cowardly" at all, but a perfectly logical and sound outcome. Any army not fighting strictly for physical survival would retreat when it recognized the deadly superiority of the enemy's weapons. Under the circumstances, the desire of individual Egyptian soldiers to seek their personal safety rather than die uselessly makes perfect sense: they followed their survival instinct.

On the other hand, the Israeli army, on top of its extensive military training, was also desperately fighting for the survival of its people and country. It had to fight and win—there was no other choice.

Just six years later, in 1973, to overcome the trauma of the previous defeats and, more specifically, of the mistakenly termed "cowardly retreat," the Egyptian army, even though it was unsure it would win, had to return to the battlefield to show its courage, valor, and military ability. And the Israeli army, lulled by its supposed invincibility, let down its guard and suffered heavy losses. The Egyptians saved their honor and consequently, Egyptian President Anwar Sadat was able to reach out for peace from a place of strength and dignity. The cost was, however, another war.

The Trauma Vortex Among the Palestinians

If we apply the concepts of instinctive survival and the trauma vortex to the present situation between the Israelis and Palestinians, we can recognize the trauma of both peoples as it plays out.

Firstly, the complexity of the two opposing narratives is manifested by the very different names Palestinians and Israelis give to the same events in their respective histories. For example, the 1948 war is called the Nakbah, or the Great Catastrophe, by the Palestinians, and the War of Independence by the Israelis; the 1973 war is known as the Yom Kippur War in Israel and in the West and the

War of Ramadan in the Arab world; the 1967 Arab-Israeli war is called the Six Day War by the Israelis and the War of the Setback among the Arabs (in other words it was not a "defeat"); the uprising of 2000 is called the Intifada Al Aqsa by the Palestinians and the Palestinian Terror Campaign by the Israelis.

In Modern Times

The great Palestinian trauma is the loss of the 1948 War, when the Arabs refused to let foreign powers dictate the division of Palestine into two states and the surrounding Arab countries engaged in a war against the nascent Israeli and Jewish state. This trauma kept being re-ignited again and again by the subsequent Arab losses of the 1956 and 1967 wars against Israel; by the fact that the Palestinians were left in refugee camps—deemed necessary in order to maintain their legal status as refugees; by their feelings of helplessness around being unable to control their destinies under Egyptian and Jordanian rule; and by feelings of greater despair under Israeli rule.

The Palestinians are fighting for the land they lost and for their national identity. Furthermore, the Arab culture places much honor on the land: "Al ardh hiye al a ardh" (land is honor). When land is lost or taken away, honor is trampled underfoot and there is a greater willingness to die in order for that honor to be restored.

In addition, their daily livelihood has been at the mercy of a political process the individual Palestinian can barely influence. Their leaders have given them hope with promises impossible to keep. Too many of their children have been reared in poverty, and schooled in the need for revenge.

The majority in the United Nations, attempting to help the Palestinians by siding with them, only exacerbated the mistrust and fear of the Israelis, and made compromise more difficult to reach by passing a great number of resolutions in the Security Council against Israel only.

Furthermore, the Palestinian situation today is intrinsically linked to the Arab historical vortex of trauma that goes as far back as the threat of the Crusades and includes domination first by the Ottoman Empire and later by the European colonial powers. For all Arabs the history of the last few hundred years or so is a trauma of deep hurt, defeat, and humiliation. The Palestinians in particular felt robbed of dignity and had no control over their destiny.

Their trauma is further tied in to a global community dominated by Western thought, values, and economies, which is sometimes dismissive or unaware of Arab and Muslim culture. The Arabs view their culture as valuing faith, piety, and respect and hospitality and family. They value community over personal ambition, the heart versus the law, the personal versus the abstract and theoretical, unity and connection over autonomy.

The influence of the factors above make the case of Palestinian violence a perfect example of trauma vortex in action, attempting to redress a perceived wrong and reestablish some measure of power and justice. But, as with all actions driven in this way, solutions that come from the urge to reenact lead to further trauma and destructiveness. This often manifests in the tremendous price some of them pay in sacrificing their children's lives and subverting their most cherished family values, not to mention border closures and occupation with all the consequences that entails.

Both the 1987–1993 Intifada and the current ongoing uprising, however tragic, can be used, in their own way, to reestablish a sense of pride and dignity among the Palestinians after such a deep loss of control. Having the power to inflict fear and losses on a militarily more powerful adversary may be important to the Palestinians' sense of positive self-identity and self-esteem, restoring their honor and dignity, despite severe costs to their own safety, autonomy, infrastructure, and economy.

One possible way out of the destructive trauma vortex is if the knowledge of their own power to harm were to allow the Palestinians to reach out for another type of resolution to the political impasse in much the same way that Egyptian president Anwar Sadat did. Relying on the clear support of all the world's leaders for an independent Palestinian state, they may well be able to take the lead and be the ones to offer Israel security and the right to live in peace.

Most Israelis, however assailed by fears about their future, are determined to see that Israel survives. But they also believe that whether they do so in peace and security depends entirely on Arab and Palestinian acceptance of their country.

The Trauma Vortex Among the Israelis

The Israelis' trauma vortex is even more complex, is deeply rooted in Jewish history, and goes far back. Their trauma is the trauma of Jews around the world. Jews have been oppressed, expelled, raped, uprooted, and killed over the centuries. They have been fighting against prejudice (and at times internalizing it) in their host countries where they were the scapegoats and stigmatized as greedy, evil, part of an international conspiring cabal, and killers of God.

They lost six million in the Holocaust, after having lived through centuries of pogroms in Europe. Jews everywhere feel profound despair and rejection when they remember that most of the world did not answer to their cries for help during the Holocaust. Today they waiver between wanting to hope and trust at any cost and the intense hopelessness and fear of survival re-triggered when memories of their genocide is reawakened by a virulent resurging anti-Semitism in Europe and anti-Jewish propaganda in the Muslim world.

Their mistrust was reinforced when, from 1947 on, the Sephardic Jews were expelled or fled *en masse* from most Arab countries as a result of Arab hostility, due to the U.N. partition of Palestine into two states. The still operative declaration by many Arab states (including some Palestinians) of their intent to fight for the demise of the Jewish state perpetuates Israeli fear of survival. If facts on the ground ever support it—guarantees of full "normalization" of diplomatic, economic, and cultural relations—the recent Saudi offer of full recognition of the Israeli state in exchange for Israel pulling back to its 1967 borders could provide a basis for negotiation and help allay the Israelis' fears.

Israelis focus on the fact that they fought four wars of survival in Israel's fifty-four years of existence and face ongoing terrorism. They see themselves dealing with a United Nations they believe is still polarized by Christian anti-Semitism, economical and political opportunism, and Muslim anti-Israeli and anti-Jewish sentiment. In the same way that Jews were a minority in their host countries, Israelis see themselves as a minority nation amongst the nations of the world, still isolated and fighting to represent their interests against the influence of twenty-four Arab and fifty-six Muslim countries in the international community.

Israelis viewed the creation of Israel as their return to the Biblical land—religious or cultural—where they had always had a presence; a land they believed had not legally and officially belonged to any local nation since the exile of the Jews. This outraged the local Muslim population, which made up around 50 to 60 percent of the half million people living in Palestine at the turn of the century. Israelis still do not understand that Palestinians viewed the land itself as more significant than the notion of "nation."

Israelis had to forge a new identity, a new language, and a new culture. They had to fight for survival and create a haven for the refugees of the Holocaust and absorb the newly displaced Middle Eastern Jews.

In Israel, for the first time in the last two thousand years, Jews can exercise their instinct for physical survival other than by preventive fleeing or immigrating. But the fabric of their society has been torn in agonized soul searching triggered by their use of force during Palestinian uprisings, the war in Lebanon, and the need to control a hostile population. They waver between the readiness to facilitate a Palestinian state and being haunted by the dread and suspicion that it will be used against them.

During the second Intifada, they believe they are facing a most absurd situation in that they are vilified for having closed their borders to Palestinian workers and having created checkpoints to protect their civilians from relentless suicide-attacks. The closures hurt their economy as well as the Palestinians'. They believe they are being accused of creating a two-tier system, while they think it is in response to the continuing hostility toward their existence as an independent state. They think they are being blamed for a situation they do not have the power to change and that they are stuck in circumstances out of their control.

At the same time, they find themselves struggling with a hostile world opinion due, they believe, to a media misconception—and at times even distortion—of their role as a local power. Because anti-Semites have used the Zionist state as an excuse to attack, vilify, and persecute Jews, Israelis have been reluctant to hear any criticism that does not come within a clear context of undeniable support for their existence and their right for safety.

Furthermore, the relentlessness of the suicide-bombings and Israeli perception that the violence is deeply rooted, supported, and funded by powerful and oil-rich Arab states calling for their demise have driven most Israelis, including many in the peace camp, to feel hopeless about ever reaching an understanding between the two populations.

Israelis think the traumas they have suffered are made even more difficult to deal with since they have to both secure their physical survival and try to maintain ethical and moral standards appropriate for a democratic state. Israelis, and Jews worldwide, are finding this a very difficult dilemma.

This problem has affected their internal society. The fifty-four-year-old impasse between the Israelis and Palestinians has polarized the Jewish world in and outside of Israel into two camps, each vying to protect the issue they believe most relevant: the need to survive physically and ethically. The effect of the latest Palestinian violence may have been to help the two camps, who are dominated by these compelling preoccupations, come together instead of splitting the fabric of Israeli society. If they clearly understand the need to come together and do so, this will allow Israelis to accomplish the balancing act so crucial for their psychological and physical survival. They will be able to assert their unquestionable right to protect themselves without guilt; but they will do it within an ethically driven concern for the humanity and basic needs of their adversary—with protective use of force and no punitive or retaliatory actions. They need to keep open the doors for dialogue and compromise and continue to reach out to the moderate Arabs and Palestinians.

Today, with their identity well forged, most Israelis realize they need to recognize that the Palestinians have their own identity. Most Israelis do not feel responsible for the origin of the conflict, but they know and have accepted that they have to deal with the fact that their presence as Israelis in the Middle East has re-triggered the Arab trauma vortex. They know they need to make room for another nation and facilitate its well being.

The Role of the Third Party

On the cross-cultural front, there are daunting obstacles between the two peoples. The issue of trust, the different rules for dialogue and discourse they each follow, and their divergent views with regard to honor and the importance of individual life are vastly rooted in their religiously and culturally defined emotional make-ups. Nations of the world who want to positively contribute to the resolution of this conflict need to pay attention to the underlying traumas as well as recognize their cross-cultural differences and help them find the universal themes they have in common.

Outsiders need to understand that trauma at times forces people to fulfill their needs in destructive ways, satisfying one need at the expense of other basic needs. The international community needs to help nations and groups in conflict recognize when they are meeting needs in destructive ways.

It is possible, for example, to help Israelis read the increasing numbers in the Palestinian polls supporting suicide-bombings as an indication of the inexorable pull of the trauma vortex, fed by the ongoing cycle of violence-trauma-violence as much as by the unleashing of Jihad. As Palestinian psychologist Dr. Marwan Dwairy writes in his article *On Fear and Honor in the Conflict,* "not everyone who identifies with attacks by a *shaheed* actually means it; a great many people find themselves taking this position as a response to the injury that has been done to Palestinian national and individual dignity and honor."

It will be also helpful to show Palestinians that the more suicide-bombings, the more Israelis will respond with incursions into Palestinian territories, and the more Palestinian honor and dignity will suffer. It becomes a vicious circle in which the more they send suicide-bombers to defend their honor and regain a sense of control, the more fearful the Israelis get, reacting by trying to control the Palestinians. In the same vein, the more Israelis are fearful for their safety, the more they create checkpoints and settlements, causing the Palestinians to feel oppressed and disabused and causing them to attack. As a result, Israelis feel they have to create new settlements or expand existing ones and some talk of the need for a Greater Israel.

These two scenarios perfectly illustrate the uncontrollable escalation created by the trauma vortex, in which the boundaries between victim and victimizer get utterly blurred, and victims end up perpetuating their own victimization.

Thus, it behooves everyone truly interested in the well being of Palestinians to avoid playing on the Israelis' existential fear, "a sincere and authentic anxiety over Jewish survival . . . the anxiety is real and [that] providing security for Jews in Israel is a Palestinian interest," recognizes Dwairy. Otherwise the Israelis, feeling totally isolated and threatened, will keep pushing their governments for knee-jerk, short-term security measures. Often these fears destabilize their political system and make it very difficult for their leaders who already have to deal with a complex and difficult political system. No Israeli leader has time to stabilize his government long enough to achieve security and to give enough time to the search for creative solutions to a most daunting problem.

It also behooves everyone truly interested in the well being of Israel to attend to the despairing Palestinian situation and help them rebuild and develop their infrastructures rather than their weapons. Palestinians need to be reassured of their right to a national identity and territory. However much they seem to have been able to tug at the heart of humanity and enlist the world's sympathy to their cause, the complexity of the forces involved in the conflict has still not allowed their needs to be fulfilled. It is as if the world is invested in keeping them as a symbol of the underdog and the Israelis as a symbol of the preferred nation.

A secure and reassured Jewish state might be able to integrate these two main preoccupations: access to a stable government with the unequivocal right to defend itself within the context of spiritual/ethical survival. Of course this requires that they deal in fairness with the Palestinians and the Israeli Arabs. A stable Israel may also have more money to develop infrastructures for all its citizens and participate in conjoint ventures with its neighboring populations.

Understanding the nature of survival instincts and the impact of psychological trauma and its reenactments, as well as recognizing the urgent need to process trauma at national levels, can inform solutions for peace. It becomes more urgent every day to bring this knowledge to the international community. Trauma vortexes develop before our eyes, risking death and destruction.

Trauma vortexes are fed by so many confluent winds that they will leave no place in the world untouched. We have developed ever more sophisticated biological and germ warfare, besides nuclear weapons, and we have developed communication networks that allow mere individuals to create much havoc. It requires that voices of moderation and moral clarity take precedence for all parties concerned. It requires that the media prominently feature these voices of moderation.

How Can the International Community Help?

Governments and international media need to understand how easily the trauma vortex can be instigated when unconsciously fanned. The pull of the trauma response is hypnotic. Trauma reenactments have often spun over many generations and have made entire nations and cultures act out violently. The intense feelings that trauma generates, allied with tribal conflicts, economical hardships, ethnic and religious differences, and threats to national interests, render large social groups more susceptible to violent, irrational behavior. Trauma creates disconnection, making it easier to externalize the "other" and blame him for one's unresolved distress. It becomes easy to dissociate from the pain one causes the "other." But when revenge is chosen as a response, people simply end up participating in furthering their own traumatization. Governments can help nations recognize they are caught in the hypnotic pull.

What would have happened at the 2001 Durban Conference on Racism, Racial Discrimination, Xenophobia, and Related Intolerance if the United Nations leaders had already understood what the trauma vortex is and what needs to be done to stop it instead of being pulled by it or being helpless in face of it? For days the Conference, despite a full agenda of racial problems all over the world, turned into a row over the Middle East. Israel, the U.S., and several other countries viewed the extremist Arab countries' attempts to politicize the meeting as an effort to delegitimize the State of Israel by equating Zionism with racism and singling out the Palestinian issue while the Arabs believed they had a legitimate forum to attract world attention to their cause. The 160 delegates had to meet a ninth extra day, the U.S. and Israeli delegates walked out in protest, and the leaders of the Conference struggled to stop a conference against racism from turning into a conference promoting racism.

Would the Durban Conference have ended differently if the Arabs and their supporters had not been caught in their trauma vortex and if the Israelis and their supporters had not reacted to it, creating a conference that reflected the exact characteristics it wished to fight against? Would it have been different if the trauma-aware conference leaders had shown the participants how the two parties were feeling delegitimized and dehumanized or dismissed and insulted? If they had been able to refrain from taking sides, legitimize both, reassure them, and create a forum that would allow both to be heard and feel validated without having to invalidate each other? Would it have been different if they had recognized and called attention to clear signs of trauma vortex in action already in the wording of documents and other incidents, such as thousands of South Africans demonstrating against Israel with anti-Semitic slogans?

What would have happened if Peter Levine, specialist in trauma, had succeeded in his trip to Washington? He had traveled to the capital, hoping to warn President Clinton not to return the Serbs to Albania without some preemptory healing efforts first. He did not succeed in his attempts to reach the President. As he had anticipated, the traumatized Kosovo population, which had had no opportunity to process its individual and collective Serbian-inflicted traumas, slaughtered their returning neighbors.

Nations caught in the trauma vortex are in desperate need of help; they need the international community and the help of what Staub calls the "bystander" nations to learn to recognize the presence of the traumatic energy, to let it run its course without acting it out, or succumb to the urge to retaliate in punitive ways rather than defensive ways. Groups caught in the vortex need help to focus on how life was before it engulfed them. They need to resolve their trauma at the national level. This can be done through a concerted effort to deactivate what I call "the collective nervous system," releasing the traumatic stress in people's bodies and minds. By introducing a greater awareness of the effects of trauma and deactivation techniques to schools, clinics, and hospitals, to policymakers and the general public through media channels, workshops, and the like, we are working with the collective nervous system in such a manner that it can create a foundation that will support and sustain international resolutions calling for peace.

All resources must be used to allay fears, prevent panic and despair, restore hope, and curtail the desire for revenge. Witness the government of Sri Lanka, which ordered its soldiers who were traumatized from fighting against the fierce Tamils to undergo treatment. They needed support to contain their traumatic reactions. The Sri Lankan authorities know that a serious rise in domestic violence has marred the return of too many war veterans. Validation of suffering and of grievances, trauma awareness, and treatment are helpful; and forums that allow national distress to be aired can be crucial. The South African Truth Commission and the Rwandan Ganacas are similar efforts at addressing the traumatic dimensions of a conflict's aftermath.

Anyone intent on helping resolve the threatening Israeli-Palestinian conflict must meet both people and both traumas with deep compassion and understanding, while taking a firm stance against actions inspired by the trauma vortex on both sides. A proactive stance would be to rehabilitate the demonized elements, to legitimize the elements neglected, invalidated, or marginalized. It is not a simple task. Trauma vortexes do not go unnoticed by people witnessing them: everyone gets caught at some level. It is not in vain that the justice system attempts to choose a jury that has not been exposed to the case being judged. No one stays objective.

Furthermore, the role of "bystanders" is crucial in giving the green or the red light to the trauma vortex. Bystanders that stay passive in the face of propaganda or violence, or supportive of violence as a means to obtain political gains, encouraging the development of the vortex. Sanctions, complaints, and calls for awareness might help awaken governments and nations from their negative trance and engage them in the healing vortex. There have been occasions where, when the trauma vortex is truly out of control, force was necessary to stop it, as Staub suggests in his analysis of evil in *The Roots of Evil*. It is a counterintuitive understanding that challenges our notion of peace but that may however be necessary to save many more lives.

In the case of the Palestinian-Israeli conflict, each bystander, individual, organization, or outside nation must recognize whether they have, themselves, already been caught in the Middle East trauma vortex by favoring one side over the other. It requires that they analyze the economical, religious, political, historical, and cultural considerations that are influencing them. It requires that they understand how to extricate themselves from the trauma vortex, if they recognize they have been pulled by it.

Many of these vortexes have existed, and still do, throughout the world and throughout history. The trauma vortex is a phenomenon in the history of mankind like tornadoes and hurricanes. It is not particular to specific nations, though certain cultural characteristics—strong respect for authority, devaluation of others, and an overly superior and/or vulnerable self-concept—added to certain societal characteristics, such as prolonged deprivation, frustration of expectations, widespread criminal violence, and rapid changes in culture and society, might facilitate the development of a violent trauma vortex, as Staub indicates in *The Roots of Evil*. However, this particular Middle East vortex has riveted the world's attention because it involves many vortexes simultaneously overlapping each other: an internal vortex within Israel itself, one within the Palestinian people, one between the Israelis/Jews and Palestinians and Arabs, one between the Jews and anti-Semites around the world, one between fundamentalist Islam and the West, and very possibly one between the developed countries and the Third World countries. I believe addressing the complexity and the overlapping of these vortexes, which goes beyond the scope of this book, will allow this conflict to find resolution and allow humanity to be better, safer, and more caring.

4

THE URGE TO REPEAT:
THE PULL OF THE TRAUMA VORTEX

As we have seen with the Middle East situation, the urge to reenact trauma has major implications for society. Though we'd like to think that "time heals all wounds," often trauma persists especially if memories have not been integrated or accepted as part of one's past. Instead, the traumatic event exists as if in the present, independent of other experiences, with a life of its own. Traumatized individuals relive memories with the same intensity as if the event were repeatedly occurring in the present. Replayed incessantly, these images add more distress and sensitization until their effects become difficult to reverse. This repetition forms a destructive learning loop that can result in hyperalertness and hyperarousal. It can create paranoia, impair our ability to discriminate between stimuli, and set the stage for reenactment.

> The compulsive urge to repeat trauma is one of its most frustrating, disturbing, and dangerous aspects.

Reenactment is an unconscious attempt of the nervous system to achieve resolution. Experiencing and confronting trauma helps us learn what to avoid, and how to protect ourselves. The reenactment is really an attempt to seek completion and mastery of unresolved traumatic situations, but it is unlikely to accomplish those positive ends, as we have seen in previous chapters. Instead, it perpetuates and deepens the cycle of pain. Because completion cannot be achieved, the nervous system stays stuck in a hyperaroused state, unable to discharge the excess energy and its associated thoughts, feelings, and behaviors. Only awareness and consciousness can break the cycle of reenactment. Only discharging the energy can reestablish the balance in the nervous system and stop the need for reenactment.

VARIOUS MANIFESTATIONS OF REENACTMENT

At the individual level

The drive for reenactment is a major factor in the perpetuation of trauma. Sometimes the reenactment is blatant: one of my clients came in with a history of seven car accidents, another was raped several times, and another broke his knee once a year for the last five years, and yet another had impregnated nine women and had them abort, after his wife had left him a year after their baby was born. Consider Peter, the Vietnam veteran who became involved in a bar brawl on July 5 and was subsequently arrested. An observant officer noticed that this was the seventh time in fifteen years that Peter had been arrested for one reason or another on July 5. Further inquiry revealed that Peter had been in the trenches in Vietnam on July 5, 1968, with his best buddy when a bomb exploded. His friend's head landed on his lap. The unresolved trauma was still in Peter's nervous system. The recreated troubles were his unconscious attempts to resolve this undischarged energy.

At other times, the reenactment is indirect: a sexually molested girl may become promiscuous or be drawn to the sex industries; combat soldiers may join police swat teams; or abused women may be attracted to abusive men. Even more tragically, this drive for reenactment also contributes to the escalation and perpetuation of violent behavior. At times abused and traumatized children grow up to become perpetrators and violent offenders, abusers, or self-mutilators.

At the level of nations

The same drive for repetition that plagues individuals also plagues traumatized nations and keeps them reenacting wars and ethnic conflicts. The causes of societal trauma—famine, ethnic cleansing, wars, political, cultural and religious polarization, and oppression—frequently result in entire populations of traumatized individuals. This gives rise to feelings of powerlessness, helplessness, rage, and despair, which prepares a fertile field for oppressive regimes and disturbed and trauma-affected leaders. Traumatized social groups often organize their identities around revenge, leading to further ethnic strife, civil war, and war between nations.

Trauma disconnects people from themselves: they are caught in fear and anxiety or they feel numb and lose their critical sense. Therefore, they may act out, externalizing their feelings of violation by committing violence on others. Violence becomes an option, and often seems the only solution, because trauma disconnects people from others and from their spirituality. When people lose these connections, it becomes easy to demonize and to dehumanize "the other." (The Oklahoma City bomber provides us an extreme example of an individual disconnected from his countrymen.) It becomes easy to believe in the right of seeking to reestablish justice for one's trauma through revenge and violence. From there to committing all kind of atrocities, it is but a small step. Whole nations can become disconnected from their neighbors, demonizing them and feeling righteous about the atrocities committed against them, in war. Historically, we have many examples of the trauma vortex in action. The Hundred Years War between England and France provides a classic example of a full-blown trauma vortex that lasted a century. Sierra Leone has been trapped in its own vortex for decades—largely over control of its most precious export, diamonds—that escalated in a 1991 civil war, with tens of thousands killed, maimed, or missing.

The present ongoing struggles between Catholics and Protestants in Northern Ireland; the Israelis and Palestinians; the Serbs, Croats, and Bosnians in Eastern Europe; the Tutsis and Hutus in Rwanda; the Pakistanis and Indians in Kashmir, the Hindus and Muslims in India all have the same character. Unresolved trauma creates a vortex in which each act of violence on one side sparks another act of violence from the other side into an ever-escalating spiral of chaos, pain, and destruction.

Serbia may be a clear recent example of unresolved trauma being reignited. In 1989, Serbia commemorated its six hundred-year-old 1389 defeat in Kosovo Polje, the "cradle of Serbian culture" and symbol of courage, national honor, and holy ground, at the hands of the Ottoman Empire. This commemoration set the stage for the revitalization of the fears of loss of territory. It did not help that the Serbian leader, Slobodan Milosevic, revived the never-forgotten Serb ambitions for a Greater Serbia; these ambitions were dashed once again when Kosovo and Vojvodina demanded greater rights and participation and were declared autonomous in 1974, with the right to veto changes in the Serbian constitution.

Furthermore, their trauma vortex had already been reawakened in the twentieth century when these ethnically diverse populations were at each other's throats. World War II, in particular, saw hundreds of thousands of Serbs massacred or sent to concentration camps when Croats and Muslims sided with the Third Reich; thousands of Croats were also massacred. The troubled Serb leader, himself a product of intense personal trauma (the suicide of his parents), was able to ignite the unresolved trauma of his people by continuously replaying traumatic images from World War II on television.

Caught in the trauma vortex and its spiral of fear, terror, paranoia, and rage, the Serbs began reenacting their war traumas and, in face of Muslim opposition and rebel mujahadeens, lost all sense of perspective and took revenge. In the true spirit of the trauma vortex, they relived the humiliation of losing their power and their hopes for a Greater Serbia when Croatia and Slovenia asserted their autonomy and turned their rage on the ethnic and religious groups they felt had traumatized them decades or centuries earlier, forgetting that they had been living with these same people in relative peace for decades. A macabre detail of reenactment was sticking their enemies' decapitated heads on spears, just as was done under the Ottoman Empire.

Eventually the trauma vortex runs its course—though it will just lie dormant if it's not dealt with constructively as in Serbia—but not before leaving untold destruction and suffering in its wake. How long the vortex lasts depends on the momentum behind it, the depth of the unresolved trauma, the amount of present frustration and unmet needs of the populations under its spell, its impact on the global community, and the subsequent interventions of outside forces.

We cannot afford to let trauma vortexes start spiraling unbeknownst to us; we cannot let the momentum of trauma accelerate once we have been able to identify them. As previously noted, several trauma vortexes are spinning simultaneously: some taking shape in front of our eyes in the Arab-Islamic world; others in the West in regards to Arabs and Muslims; another between First World and Third World countries, polarizing in the pro- and anti-globalization forces. Some are continuing, including the vortex within Israeli society, the one within Palestinian society, and the one already in full force in the Middle East between Arabs/Palestinians and Israelis. Some are reawakening, like the one spinning worldwide in regards to anti-Semitism. These will leave unimaginable mayhem and devastation if we let them develop or feed them unwittingly.

The truth is, any nation can eventually escape the trauma vortex. Often the vortex runs out of steam when people are no longer willing to pay the price of its aftermath or when other powers intervene. And yet, again, it may just lie latent if the real issues are not addressed constructively.

THE MEDIA AND THE RELATIONSHIP BETWEEN TRAUMA AND VIOLENCE

Once the media understands the relationship between trauma and violence, it will be able to shift (if it so desires) the context of portraying society, crime, abuse, war, violence, and terrorism.

> Understanding the biological underpinning of trauma and violence can reshape our understanding of political conflicts. It can usher in a new political dialogue, a rethinking of education and social programs, an accounting of the unfathomable costs of trauma, and a global commitment to healing trauma.

Many psychological, physiological, and behavioral effects of trauma and the relationship between trauma and the media were covered in Chapters 2 and 5. Here I will focus briefly on the relationship between trauma and violence for two reasons: first, because violence figures so prominently in public attention, and secondly, because so many people place blame on the media.

It is important to emphasize that most people who are traumatized do not become outwardly violent. Still, numerous studies have demonstrated that many adults and children who have been traumatized do turn their aggression against others. Bessel van der Kolk explains, "Reenactment of victimization is a major cause of violence in society." Studies of violent criminals have shown that extremes of childhood trauma and abuse are always present in their histories.

WHY HISTORY REPEATS ITSELF

When people are traumatized, their internal system remains aroused and this arousal sends signals of threat. Always on edge, unable to relax, they are constantly aware of a pervading sense of danger and suspicious of everything and everyone. Failing to grasp the source and reason for their discomfort, their fear escalates. This, in turn, amplifies a need to identify the source of the threat, which they project outside of themselves.

The vast majority of traumatized people "act in," turning their terror, rage, and shame inward. This systematically undermines their health and sense of well being, manifesting in depression, apathy, and low self-esteem. However, it is common, even for those people, to have sudden bursts of "acting out" followed by feelings of deep remorse and self-degradation over what they've done.

Acting Out

A young woman named Paula waits for the bus, at six o'clock in the evening, when, unexpectedly, a homeless person walks back and forth in front of her, eyeing her and muttering crazy words. Paula's glazed eyes followed him warily, but she remains still, her body rigid and frozen. She enters the crowded bus and sits next to two teenagers who attempt to manhandle her. She then pulls a gun from her pocket and shoots them both.

Six months prior to this incident, Paula, a personal trainer, had been robbed at gunpoint on an empty bus. She was so severely hurt that she had to abandon her training career after undergoing several back surgeries. After her tragedy she had purchased a revolver, intent on defending herself if the need should again arise—and she thought it did.

If we look at this scenario from the trauma vortex perspective, we see the image of a severely traumatized woman. Her distant look is a clue of her dissociation, her leaving her body. Dissociation is a key symptom of trauma. It has been shown to be the single most important predictor of chronic PTSD.

When the crazy man paced in front of her, Paula was already on alert. Her hyperaroused physiology warned her of imminent danger and her irrational mind took over. She was hyperalert and her eyes focused narrowly on the man's strange behavior, also evidence of trauma. Her nervous system was now on hair-trigger alert when she entered the bus. The undischarged energy still stuck in her body from the time of her attack was driving her actions.

The defensive response that she was powerless to execute when she was assaulted exploded in full force. Trapped in the bus, she couldn't flee; her only option was to follow the urge of her instinct to fight, in the hope that it would help her discharge the powerful survival energy still stuck in her body. To her psyche, no time had passed since the assault, as if she were frozen in time, the traumatic event still happening in the present.

Caught in the pull of the trauma vortex, she did not avoid the threatening teenagers, but sat next to them, a moth drawn to the flame, pulled toward the vortex of violence. The teenager closer to her made a move toward her and spoke to her. Driven by her rage, Paula pulled the trigger several times, obliterating the perceived threat. As the bus doors opened Paula walked calmly away, in a trance.

Many women in prison convicted of murder and manslaughter have similar stories to Paula's. Only the awareness of an etiology of violence rooted in trauma can help understand these women and alleviate their plight as well as that of countless traumatized people.

An Instinct for Justice

From a biological perspective, Paula's actions were a powerful and compelling example of reenactment and fall into the category of survival defenses. How can dangerous reenactments that plague many traumatized individuals and societies have a survival value?

In his thought-provoking book *Violence*, psychiatrist James Gilligan makes the profound statement that "the attempt to achieve and maintain justice, or to undo or prevent injustice, is the one and only universal cause of violence." He sees violence not just as violence, but the story of relations between family members and between different groups, ethnicities, races, and nations; he understands violence to be a means of resolving conflicts. It is, however, an always-tragic way to do so.

Violence leads to retaliation and punishment and these in turn lead to aggravation of violence, to its perpetuation instead of deterring it. "Violence includes the lives of the victimizers and the victims," says Gilligan. Evermore, victims become perpetrators and perpetrators become victims.

Peter Levine, who learned from his studies of animal behaviors about the biological level of trauma, offers another option. He describes that, physically, a sense of justice can be experienced as discharge and completion. Without discharge and completion of the traumatic energy, we are bound to repeat the tragic cycle of violent reenactment, in our driven search for a sense of justice.

Much of humanity appears to be fascinated by those of us who act out our search for justice. Many successful books and movies detail the lives of serial killers and revenge seekers. Underlying our powerful attraction to those who act out is the urge for completion and resolution—or what Peter Levine calls "renegotiation" of trauma. The movie *In the Bedroom,* based on a true story, is a perfect example of the trauma vortex seeking revenge in the name of justice. The highly acclaimed movie describes the story of Matt and Ruth Fowler, whose son Frank is killed by Richard, the abusive and brooding ex-husband of Frank's older girlfriend. Richard's family runs their little town in Maine, making it possible for him to skirt the law. The movie portrays Matt and Ruth's slow descent into despair and the inexorable pull of the trauma vortex, which makes this perfectly normal husband and father seek justice, with the unspoken acceptance of his wife, by premeditating and executing Richard's murder—to avenge Frank's death.

But when we "renegotiate" trauma, in other words, when we heal it, the repetitive cycle of violent reenactment is transformed, and with it the need for revenge or violence disappears. Shame and blame dissolve in the powerful wake of renewal and self-acceptance. However, what occurs in movies like *In the Bedroom,* in which the father commits the murder, gets away with it, and continues to live a normal life, doesn't necessarily reflect everyday reality. Does violent reenactment resolve the trauma? Does it achieve justice? We have seen that it does not. If that were the case, there would be no need for the repeated attempts to discharge and complete thwarted survival responses that characterize most people who act out violently. There would be far fewer serial killers and so-called vigilante avengers. After only one violent act, most people's nervous systems could normalize and they would go on with their lives. But, in fact, there is a lack of integration between the three parts of the brain. The action has not been decided from a fully integrated place. Thus the social cost is tremendous, as violence engenders more violence.

When it is not physically possible for a traumatized individual to completely discharge the intense energies that are mobilized as a protective mechanism by the body, the residual effects may be experienced as terrifying and compulsive flashbacks that are akin to reliving the event, or as rage and/or obsessive thinking. The nervous system remains highly activated, which compels him to seek the only relief he knows—more violence, however temporary that relief it brings may be. The traumatic event is not resolved, and the individual continues to behave as if it is still happening—because, biologically speaking, it is.

We also need to consider cultural differences, from civilization to civilization. Western countries have officially put justice in the hands of civil law and removed it from the responsibility or the right of individuals. In other societies, however, it is not only socially approved but maybe even required to take justice into one's hands. There can be, understandably, a serious culture clash between two societies that operate at such different levels and much tragedy can ensue from such lack of understanding.

Social and Global Consequences

The most recent research on trauma raises critical questions concerning the potential damage caused to future generations of children ravaged by abuse, neglect, war, and violence.

It is imperative that we learn to successfully treat the effects of trauma. We may be unintentionally spawning hyperactive, learning-impaired, and violence-prone citizens. Solving this threat to local and global social stability remains one of our greatest challenges.

In areas where external threat is an everyday reality (such as the inner city and war zones), the combination of undischarged internal survival responses, poverty, and life-threatening circumstances create explosive and self-perpetuating situations. The formation of urban and rural gangs (including cults and militias) has its root in instinctual survival behavior. But without the tools for renegotiation, the actions of these groups are limited to withdrawal from society and/or violent reenactment. Due to the synergistic effect of intense feelings and the rules of mass psychology, groups, including alienated gangs, warring tribes, ethnic/religious communities, and nations, are extremely susceptible to violent and irrational behaviors.

The Collective Trauma Vortex

Trauma is a universal condition; everyone is vulnerable to it. Cultures pass on their historical traumatic events through literature and art. Cave paintings depict life-and-death confrontations with predators. The Bible is full of disaster, violence, and tragedy, as are the myths of most cultures. In the traditional hero's journey, the pursuit of an ideal requires the hero to first descend to the underworld, successfully encounter a dangerous situation, and gain some quality of mastery in order to survive. Humankind may well be defined by our ability to learn and to tell stories. So it has always been.

But something has happened over the last one hundred years to change our relationship to storytelling. Even in the early twentieth century, a resident of a village or small town might be touched by a few calamities per year—family conflicts or sickness, a flood, a fire, an explosion, perhaps murders or rapes that became public knowledge, possibly a regional or national conflict that impinged somehow on the lives of local citizens. People paid serious attention to these events. Newspapers wrote about them. But such trauma did not make up the majority of people's reality.

But during the latter half of the twentieth century, events and information became national and then global: commerce, trade, politics, technology and communications, war, and crimes against humanity. We now live in concurrent cultures in which our stories are told by global instantaneous media. Crimes and calamities in Istanbul and East Timor are witnessed and felt in little Slippery Rock, Pennsylvania. The media is a mirror. It always has been. Today it is a global mirror and a magnifying one. And it supplies the vast majority of our collective reality.

The process of dealing with traumatic stories moved from the individual into a collective trauma vortex. Once the collective consciousness is traumatized, even those not personally traumatized participate in its effects. Untold millions around the globe, their number growing every day, share in broadcast trauma. This may well generate a hunger and a compulsion to repeat and reenact. In our collective trauma vortex, too many of us suffer from chronic stress, chronic numbness, or, for some of us, deep polarization. As mirrors and storytellers, media members confront in their audiences a rising threshold of stimulation, sensation, and speed and, as they are part of the collective, they are affected as much as everyone else, and sometimes more.

5

SECONDHAND TRAUMA

Secondhand trauma might be a clue to how trauma gets generalized. Secondhand trauma, like secondhand smoke, refers to the impact trauma has on the witnesses associated with trauma victims. Also known as "vicarious traumatization" or "compassion fatigue," it arises from the simple fact that, in dealing with the fear, pain, and suffering of traumatized people, professionals and other bystanders often experience similar emotions and aftereffects themselves.

Secondhand trauma, like the trauma vortex, is also emotionally contagious. Anyone who comes in contact with a traumatized person is exposed to possible secondhand trauma, especially those on the front lines: people in the healing, helping, and protective professions such as therapists, doctors, nurses, medics, social workers, firemen and police, clergy, and emergency and disaster workers. Police, firefighters, and rescue workers, already aware of the impact of secondary trauma, have introduced the practice of debriefing as an initial attempt to diffuse harmful effects of exposure to trauma.

Charles Figley, author of *Compassion Fatigue*, proposes the diagnostic term Secondary Traumatic Stress Disorder for people suffering from secondhand trauma. Like PTSD, symptoms of STSD include re-experiencing, avoidance, and persistent arousal. Laurie

Anne Pearlman and Karen Saakvitne, authors of *Trauma and the Therapist*, see vicarious trauma as cumulative. This makes sense when one considers the repeated exposure of those in trauma's front "line of fire"—from police, to therapists, to reporters. In a 1996 study of stress in counselors in the field of trauma researchers, Marla Arvay and M.R. Uhlemann found that 14 percent reported traumatic stress levels similar to those experienced by clients with PTSD. Remarkably, this is even higher than among victims actually exposed to accidents, violent crime, and deaths, who report rates of only 7 to 11 percent.

"It is our clinical responsibility to make sure we are not harmed by our work," said Karen Saakvitne, in regards to therapists. "If we don't take care of ourselves, we can't take care of our clients." The same concept can apply to media professionals.

THE MEDIA AND SECONDHAND TRAUMA

Media members have to deal with formidable challenges meeting relentless deadline pressures and intense competition. They have to deal with complex situations that have to be grasped and digested in a very short time and re-packaged in succinct words or highly charged stories delivered in 90-second news bites. As Linda Scherzer writes in her article "The Media and the Message": "Each day, reporters, editors and their crews handle a minimum of five 30-minute videocassettes, amounting to more than two and a half hours of material." Media people, given their lifestyles alone, are already walking the line between self-care and stress-induced problems. Beyond the normal high pressures of the job, media members are often exposed to direct trauma when they witness violence and tragedy first hand, or to secondhand trauma from repetitive exposure in the aftermath of tragedy—whether through interviewing victims and perpetrators, or from the compelling images that are constantly replayed. Furthermore, many have been personally exposed to threats and beatings; colleagues may have been killed—by soldiers or governing entities angry at their reports—or died in the line of fire. "In 2000, the Committee to Protect Journalists (CPJ) documented 24 journalists killed and 81 journalists imprisoned for practicing their profession. Reporters Without Borders (RWB) indicated that 85 journalists were imprisoned since the beginning of 2001. Further, 446 news gatherers were arrested and 653 were attacked or threatened in 2000." These facts are detailed by Elana Newman, a professor and clinical psychologist specializing in psychological trauma and PTSD, in her article included in *Sharing the Front Line and the Back Hills.* This is a timely and brilliant book, written by Yael Danieli, who serves as a Senior Representative to the United Nations of the World Federation for Mental Health and of the International Society for Traumatic Stress Studies, in addition to her wide-reaching roles in the mental health field.

Media people can also be exposed to the subtle moral and psychological dilemma resulting from being coerced to report only what these entities approve of, in order to have access to information. Some may be vulnerable to the Stockholm syndrome, in which, when challenged by the difficulty of handling incongruence, it becomes easier to adopt the philosophy of the entity that threatens. This is yet another subtle way that trauma affects the very lens through which we see the world.

Indeed, there has been a growing realization in the industry that, despite long-held journalistic tradition, members of the media can hardly operate as impartial witnesses. Journalists have been trained that "it is not their job to think about themselves but to think about others. They have been trained to focus more on what has happened than on what they think and feel about it," explained Gina Barton, Dart Fellow and journalist for the *Milwaukee Journal*

Sentinel. However, Barton believes that no matter how objective they are trained to be, they are human beings with their own psyches, emotions, and personal histories, and they are far from immune to the events they report or photograph. In addition, maybe objectivity as an absolute value in journalism needs some modification. Barton said her work in Rwanda and Bosnia helped her learn that "objectivity isn't the most valuable thing; [that] a journalist needs to feel his/her feelings in order to be empathetic" and "being empathetic can assist you in being more fair." It may even be a sign of more objectivity when we recognize and accept the inevitability of our subjectivity. Maybe the change that will be welcome in the field is to "replace objectivity with fairness."

We see the world through the media's eyes, which is to say we see it through the lenses of the individual reporters, editors, and packagers of news. What kind of lenses do they wear? Is the very lens through which we perceive the world shaped by the trauma the media reports on? What happens to each media person when he/she views traumatic events day in and day out? Might not secondhand trauma be at work with media personnel, too, as a result of covering the traumatic field? Just like firefighters and police, print and video reporters, news media editors and researchers, newscasters, and camera personnel spend much time covering the fear, pain, and suffering of individuals and groups when reporting on traumatic events.

Furthermore, media people are exposed more than anyone else to the variety and intensity of man's cruelty and inhumanity toward his fellow man, in all cultures and all over the world. They take in the heartbreaking images of child soldiers and amputees, of women raped, tortured, or throwing their children over the fence of a U.N. compound, desperate to save them from starvation. "We are peeling away horrible stories," says Janine di Giovanni, in an interview with Evgenia Peretz, in *The Girls at the Front.*

The more conscious the reporter is, the more vulnerable he/she is to being traumatized. Many feel ". . . a nagging sense of guilt that they are war profiteers of a sort," writes Peretz. "We are vultures really," says di Giovanni, expressing the difficulty she has because, after their job is done, media personnel leave the trauma and war victims and get to go home. Some, like former CNN correspondent Siobhan Darrow, author of *Flirting with Danger* and former war journalist, are aware of the addictive nature of covering trauma and violence and compare war to drugs. "I had the feeling of being a junkie," says Darrow, talking about the void she felt when she stopped covering war for any length of time, whether in Albania, Chechnya, or the Balkans.

In reality, media members are continually at risk for secondhand trauma. Some may be suffering from it to the degree that is injurious to their health. The research on the traumatic stress of journalists has just begun and needs to be "ongoing and exploratory . . . pending that definitive study [is] yet to come," says Dr. Roger Simpson, Associate Professor of Communications at the University of Washington and Director of the Dart Center for Journalism and Trauma. Several studies have in fact been completed; one in particular, by Dr. Anthony Feinstein of the University of Toronto, confirms that a high percentage of war reporters suffer from depression and PTSD (28.5 percent). Although the results were that the vast majority of them were not traumatized, it detailed that one in three showed evidence of psychological distress.

Research shows that the effects of witnessing horror can be cumulative. The longer journalists are in the field, and the more they are exposed to horror, the greater their chances to develop PTSD. Fortunately, there is a fledgling awareness in the field that covering gruesome stories can create much psychological stress and that denying or "stuffing" the aftermath of trauma is likely to cause the stress to build—resulting in nightmares, flashbacks, and intrusive images. A very recent initiative, for example, is one called Newscoverage Unlimited, an organization of "mutual-support volunteers" established by Frank Ochberg and taken over by The Dart Center for Journalism and Trauma at the University of Washington. The organization is "concerned with the well being of reporters, editors, and columnists, who were traumatized as a result of covering the September 11 attacks in New York City, Washington D.C., and Somerset County, Pennsylvania," as Dirk Schouten reported in his article "Traumatic News Hurts Journalists Too."

Media people need to be aware of the risks involved in their jobs. They need to be encouraged to seek help when they recognize traumatic symptoms in themselves without risking the loss of important assignments. "It needs a lot more publicity. People need to talk about it more. Nobody knew about posttraumatic stress in soldiers . . . [but] it's now being accepted more and more that soldiers suffer from that," says BBC human rights documentary producer Giselle Portenier, who believes that European journalists are even less prepared and less warned about the psychological vulnerabilities of their jobs. Some also think that providing trauma prevention is " beyond the resources of most news organizations," and yet the need is dire.

Akila Gibbs, a television news journalist I interviewed, presents a clear example of media employees' need for support. Gibbs left her job because she could not face one more day seeking the "juiciest" of life's tragedies. "I just couldn't take it anymore," she told me. She also reflected on the pain she felt exploiting people's vulnerability by exposing their anguish—which is what her job required. She had to quit, she said, though she mourned the loss of the career that she had pursued since the age of eleven.

Gibbs is not alone in suffering the effects of highly stressful demands of the news industry. People in the business show high rates of divorce and chronic health problems including heart attacks, alcohol/drug abuse, and absenteeism. Reports, as well as clinical data from therapists, show that media people, like front-line people, suffer from traumatic symptoms such as flashbacks, nightmares, outbursts of anger and hostility, and self-destructive ideation at times culminating in suicide attempts.

One of the most tragic stories of secondhand trauma is that of South African photojournalist Kevin Carter, who won the Pulitzer Prize in 1994 for a picture taken in Sudan that "made the world weep" and became an icon of Africa's plight. The photo, published in *The New York Times,* showed a collapsed child barely alive, on her way to a feeding station, with a vulture landed in view. According to *Time* magazine, in an article by the magazine's Johannesburg bureau chief Scott Macleod, after taking the photo and chasing the bird away, Carter "sat under a tree, lit a cigarette, talked to God, and cried. He described taking that photo as "the most horrifying experience of my career." Two months after winning the prize, "his body was found in his red pickup truck; parked near a small river where he used to play as a child." He was dead of carbon monoxide poisoning.

Carter's suicide note was a litany of flashbacks, nightmares, and gloomy images, attempts at reviewing his life, analyzing himself, and apology. "I am really sorry," Carter wrote, "the pain of life overrides the joy to the point that joy does not exist." After coming home from New York, he was "depressed" and "haunted by the vivid memories of killings & corpses & anger & pain. . . of starving or wounded children, of trigger-happy madmen, often police, of killer executioners," explained his sister in a letter to *Time* magazine. "The pain of his mission, to open the eyes of the world to so many of the issues and injustices that tore at his own soul, eventually got to him. The year 1993 was a good one for him, but at the end of it he told me he really needed a break from Africa, that it was getting to him. He knew then that he was losing perspective." Kevin's suicide was the outcome of a series of events, and possibly a trauma that came over other traumas, that simply overwhelmed his nervous system and his capacity to cope.

Secondary trauma—in this case from exposure to victims and the aftermath of disaster scenes—can create traumatic symptoms even if the reporter, news editor, or photographer is doing his job from a relatively safe distance. A recent research study has also shown that the large majority of an interviewed group of media people had experienced trauma in their lives, and that more than 80 percent had witnessed violent events while on duty.

In a 1999 article in the *Columbia Journalism Review* entitled "Burnout Stress on the Job," Joanmarie Kalter documents the different forces contributing to journalists' stress burnout and the awareness that is starting to pervade the field. "Twenty years ago, if you said journalism was stressful, the response would have been, 'so what?'" John Russial, newspaper consultant and associate professor of journalism from the University of Oregon, told her. "Today, there's an increase in consciousness about its risks." As this awareness grows, the field is beginning to make changes in training among its professional ranks.

Kalter quotes the work of Roger Simpson. In 1996, Simpson surveyed 131 journalists at several newspapers in Michigan and Washington. He found that the journalists described the same degree of posttraumatic symptoms as Australian firefighters who had recently battled a brushfire and of Norwegian soldiers that had been trapped in an avalanche. Today, firefighters and soldiers routinely receive stress debriefing—a one-time counseling to air their distress—while journalists are barely starting to acknowledge theirs.

Even traumatic events that seem banal leave an impact. Simpson found, for example, that the reporters most likely to develop traumatic symptoms were those who had covered fatal car accidents. The longer the exposure to specific events, the more likely a respondent would experience avoidance tendencies and intrusive thoughts.

The September 11 tragedies brought the issues of media traumatization—which had been deeply felt by many war correspondents for years without recognition by their field at large—more sharply into focus. Mark Brayne, BBC foreign correspondent and psychotherapist, noted the shift. "Journalists are trained to be skeptical, even cynical—whether it is toward politicians, spin doctors, or indeed psychotherapists. After all, journalists report only the facts, do we not? We are objective and balanced. We are not part of the story. News is what happens outside us. But events like those of this week tell us something different. We get drawn in, and of course we are affected—sometimes profoundly—physically, emotionally, spiritually."

Brayne knows that trauma certainly does not hit everybody, but when it does it destroys careers and relationships, and more dramatically still, lives. Journalists are clearly as exposed to, and can be as affected by, trauma as the police or fireman or soldiers whose leaders have recognized the seriousness of this issue years before the journalists'. ". . . Journalists can be traumatized by our work. Trauma needs to be talked about—which is where therapy and listening come in. Today after a terrible week, there are many who will need to be heard in their grief, confusion, and shock," wrote Brayne.

Delayed Reactions

Like policemen, firemen, or soldiers, journalists "typically experience a delayed trauma reaction" triggered by some seemingly inconspicuous and unrelated incident months or years after leaving "the battlefield." As Kalter reports, during the traumatic event, correspondents "focus fiercely on the task at hand: asking questions, writing down notes, taking refuge in the distance and control their job provides; they may not even know they've been affected. Later, however, some will suffer from dread, insomnia, emotional numbing, and intense, intrusive memories that bring back the full force of their horror." *Daily Oklahoman* Managing Editor Ed Kelley explains, "Unlike anybody else in this society we're supposed to shut it all out. It's a myth, we can't do it."

Sherry Ricchiardi, in her 1999 article "Confronting The Horror," published in *American Journalism Review,* recognized that covering trauma and violence can create enormous stress for journalists and advises getting help. She describes how war photographer John Gaps, author of *God Left Us Alone Here: A Book of War,* found that macabre details haunted him long after leaving the Balkans, despite his attempts to vent his stress through poetry writing. "The image of a silver watch, for instance, on the wrist of a Serbian soldier whose head had been blown off by a rocket during the 1991 war in Croatia" was seared in his memory. "His boots were still laced up, nice and tidy, and the watch was running," Gaps recalls. "Those are the little things that take away your ability to reason later on."

Kalter quotes Donatella Lorch in a poignant interview: "After Rwanda, it took me a year before I even learned how to sleep again," said Donatella, who covered the genocide for *The New York Times.* Upon returning to Nairobi, she walked to her window and saw her gardener with a machete. "I instinctively ran to the other side of the room," she explained. "I wasn't even able to control myself . . . It stays with you, yes, it does stay with you. I left Africa and had six months of darkness in my soul, a really deep depression."

Kalter writes what Keith Miller, an NBC correspondent based in London, described to her: "You are given a countdown to 'live' requiring a very clear head . . . accompanied by a serious adrenaline rush. Three minutes later, you're down. Then you've got to come back up again. When you do that for fifteen hours or more it can be really debilitating." Miller captures the surrealistic experiences of a journalist. He notes, "easy air travel can make such experiences even more ghastly and surreal." Speaking of his coverage of Rwanda, he said, "We left Kigali and that afternoon were at a garden party in Wimbledon. People said, 'Where were you?' I just couldn't talk about it."

But some people are aware it can be different. Ricchiardi reports that Chris Cramer, currently president of CNN's international news division, "while head of newsgathering for the BBC in London, helped launch debriefing programs for journalists handling high-risk assignments." In 1980, Iranian dissidents took Cramer hostage along with twenty-five others during a siege of the Iranian Embassy in London. He was pistol-whipped and held at gunpoint. "I was a basket case for years afterwards. I came off the road because of it. Had I known more about stress and trauma, I might have gotten over it a bit faster," said Cramer. This was firsthand trauma on the job.

The case of Hilary Mackenzie, Washington Bureau Chief for Southam News, interviewed in Schouten's article, illustrates the secondhand trauma of witnessing from up close the effects of the aftermath of genocide when she was reporting from Kosovo and Sierra Leone. Mackenzie recognizes that the nightmares she still has of Sierra Leone's girls, as young as twelve years old, maimed and raped, is part of what she describes as "probably stuff built up inside of me." Mackenzie had dealt with the emotions aroused by her experience by talking with friends and family. But she also acknowledges that she may have to go for professional help.

Trauma and Stigma

Ricchiardi further quotes psychiatrist Frank Ochberg, who helped develop the Victims and Media Program at the School of Journalism at Michigan State University, who explained: "Journalists, by habit or culture, refuse to feel their grief, their horror, their anxiety." Martin Cohen, a Florida psychologist who has worked with journalists at Poynter Institute for Media Studies, cautions reporters that they are "not just an objective journalist doing your job, but a human being who has been exposed to something awful." He recommends that journalists be debriefed from twenty-four to seventy-two hours after exposure to a traumatic event.

However, Cohen points out that most journalists are unlikely to seek counseling for fear of being stigmatized. "The rank and file is not going to ask for [help]. Their hearts may be broken open even though they have the distance of being at the end of a camera lens. It is as if they are injected with a poison, a certain kind of energy that can negatively affect them for a long time if they don't deal with it, which is often the case. They fear that asking for help and support would be interpreted as a shameful weakness when in fact, it is wisdom. These are some of the consequences of witnessing the suffering of others. The mere exposure to trauma can be traumatic."

Patricia Drew, director of *The New York Times* stress-debriefing program, concurs in her interview with Joanmarie Kalter. In fact, she admits, reporters at first are reluctant to use her program's services, in which they would have the opportunity to discuss their experience and feelings. "They are afraid they won't be sent out on the next tough story," she says.

Others are more aware. In Ricchiardi's article, *Arizona Republic* reporter Karina Bland believes that traumatic events fuel her passion to write. "Because I feel [the horror] so strongly, I wrote more graphically so people could feel it," she explains. "I had to go through the suffering and put myself in a pretty awful place to do that." It took her losing fifteen pounds and hitting the bottle to self-medicate her nightmares about the burnt, beaten, murdered children in her reports before she overcame her embarrassment and sought therapy.

But Rick Bragg, *The New York Times* Pulitzer Prize-winning photographer, had a harder time taking advantage of counseling because he didn't want to identify with the role of the victims. He covered the Oklahoma City bombing, multiple murders in New Orleans, and the Jonesboro, Arkansas, student killings. "That is real hurt," he says in reference to his memories of the agonized expression of a woman whose husband was killed in Oklahoma City. "What's happened to us is so much less," he explains. "That doesn't mean what happens to us isn't serious. But I don't feel I have a right to call myself a victim. . . . I never felt it was appropriate to whine . . . we can't act like that or we can't get the job done."

Here, there's simply a need for restructuring of thought. We could say to Bragg, it's not about whining or taking on the victim status; it's about recognizing the impact of secondhand trauma because of the role that the amygdala has in trauma and the need to process what you experienced as a witness to horrifying events. If you give yourself time to acknowledge what you're feeling, then you'll be better able to continue doing your job.

According to Ricchiardi, Lindsey Hilsum, a diplomatic correspondent for Channel 4 News in London, did not seek psychological help after spending time in Rwanda because she believed no one in London would understand her experience: "What kind of counselor am I going to find in London—someone who doesn't even know were Rwanda is? [. . .] The problem isn't me: it's not in my head. I have a right to be upset about this. It was an awful, dreadful thing I witnessed."

When Hilsum says, "It's not in my head," she means she's not making it up. She assumes that because her traumatizing experience was real, not invented, there is no recovery possible. This is simply untrue. There are ways to detoxify these kinds of over-whelming experiences.

> The stigma attached to being affected by first- and secondhand trauma needs to be addressed and normalized for all of us. We must talk openly and treat trauma as we do any other disorder.

Surveys have found that nearly 40 percent of editors report job-related health problems ranging from insomnia to alcoholism and hypertension, and these numbers are on the rise. "The culture of bravado that fans the flames also discourage them from slowing down or seeking counseling," says Robert Giles, now Executive Director of the Media Studies Center in New York. "They must be seen as war-horses, impervious to trauma, fatigue, and fear." This hurts them deeply.

When journalists truly understand how secondhand trauma affects them, they may recognize how it can become difficult to represent the whole spectrum of human experience in their work. What's new and interesting is replaced by the narrow focus and single-mindedness of the trauma vortex. Can a journalist, limited by the unawareness of either his own trauma, or the pull of the trauma field he is covering, communicate the whole scope of human tragedy and traumatic experience, which must also include healing and hope? If he has shut down psychologically, he will not have access to his full range of emotions. It is helpful for reporters to also recognize that untreated personal traumas from their past might make them more vulnerable to job stress and burnout, and to reporting slanted toward the trauma vortex; that it can influence their choice of what is newsworthy and their style of coverage. Trauma is so arresting, a person's attention focuses on it automatically, even compulsively. It is obvious how reporting of the full range of life can become compromised.

Non-governmental workers and U.N. personnel also need to become aware of the impact of secondhand trauma on themselves and their judgment. Working with the victims of trauma in a war zone can make them easily pulled in by the trauma vortex of their clients and espouse the polarized beliefs and emotions of their constituents and lose their impartiality. I interviewed two American U.N. workers who served in Serbia and Kosovo. Although they were close colleagues and conversed often together, they had a very different read of the situation in Yugoslavia, each taking the side of the people they helped. This becomes a real problem when NGOs make political statements that may inform international policy. Furthermore, they are themselves often exposed to dangerous, provoking, or humiliating situations.

HELP IS ON THE WAY

The trauma vortex and its hypnotic pull biases media coverage. Reactions to secondhand trauma can be numbing of emotions, compartmentalization, fixation on traumatic events, hyperalertness, and cynicism as a result of too much exposure to human cruelty and nature's indifference to human suffering.

Reactions to secondhand trauma can infiltrate reporting and leave the viewing public feeling numb, hopeless and helpless, or in panic and dread.

Strides are being made to support and educate media professionals to take care of themselves in these areas. There is hope that, as awareness and opportunities for trauma awareness and counseling continue to grow, posttraumatic debriefing will become as natural and matter of fact as in other exposed professions.

Encouragingly, attempts to address these difficult issues in the media have been initiated as the number of casualties in the field has risen. In December 2001, panelists Sherry Ricchiardi from Indiana University at Indianapolis and Jack Saul from New York University presented a paper, "Journalists in the Aftermath of War," at the International Society for Traumatic Stress Studies Annual Convention in New Orleans. Using their survey of journalists from Croatia, Bosnia, and Kosovo as examples, Ricchiardi and Saul described the difficulties these individuals face when working under harassment, government censorship, and severe physical intimidation. Journalists wrestle daily with the impossible task of telling the truth about traumatic events in their own countries, the hostility their coverage provokes in their communities, and the danger they face in doing so.

The panel also covered the plight of journalists confronting trauma in themselves and in their sources. The team was able to offer the Balkan journalists a groundbreaking workshop called "Media and Trauma: Emotional Fallout from Covering Violence" in Croatia in January 2002. They helped reporters diffuse their anger and offered them a forum in which to air their feelings.

A similar conference is being planned in the former Soviet territories for media members covering Chechnya, Georgia, and Afghanistan. Furthermore, the International Society for Traumatic Stress Studies' website reports on preliminaries for a Dart Center cyber course on covering violence around the world. Other university journalism programs focus on training the media to deal with traumatic events. Among them is a particularly interesting one-hour documentary that was produced by a group from Colorado University, headed by Associate Dean Meg Moritz. *Covering Columbine* focused on the psychological impact of the Columbine story on all the media people who reported on it. The video has been successfully used as a training tool for professionals and students in journalism. It is being presented nationally and internationally and is available for free to journalism teachers through the Dart Center website.

WHAT TO DO ABOUT SECONDHAND TRAUMA

Participation in well-run Critical Incident Stress Debriefing (CISD) groups is one way to help resolve upsetting experiences more quickly, as long as participation is voluntary and not mandatory. According to the International Critical Incident Stress Foundation, Inc., the reporter who witnesses or experiences a so-called "critical incident" and who has no opportunity to psychologically unload, runs the risk of stress-induced ailments and PTSD. The following strategies are recommended:

- Talk to people close to you.

- Notice if you are numbing your pain with alcohol or drugs: these are ineffective long-term coping strategies.

- Understand that some recurring thoughts, dreams, or flashbacks are normal. They usually will fade over time. If they don't, this may warrant professional intervention.

- Recognize that stress is a normal reaction; don't label yourself as weak or crazy, whining, or trying to avoid it. Expand your efforts to break traditional "macho" rules of silence or of keeping a stiff upper lip.

- Know your own personal vulnerabilities and unresolved issues, as this insight helps reduce the risk for vicarious traumatization. Beth Stamm, a psychologist and Research Associated Professor at Idaho State University has created a wonderful website (http://www.isu.edu/~bhstamm) focusing on Secondary Traumatization that discusses these issues in much greater detail.

- Take time to relax, whether a few minutes or a few hours, after a stressful situation. Give yourself at least two consecutive weeks vacation every few months.

- Take care of your body with diet and exercise.

- Find a hobby or take time with family or friends.

- Beware of isolating yourself. Get involved in professional organizations where you can meet colleagues and discuss with them events and problems.

- Learn techniques to relieve stress, especially those related to breathing.

- Watch for warning signs of burnout:
    - Loss of appetite and sexual desire;
    - Overeating; use of alcohol or drugs;
    - Insomnia or sleeping too much;
    - Loss of interest in hobbies and/or loss of creativity;
    - Feeling hyperaroused or unable to focus;
    - Feeling victimized, moody, or like you're carrying the world on your shoulders;
    - Loss of meaning.

- Keep an eye out for colleagues or staff members that may show signs of being affected by trauma, and encourage or support them to seek help.

If you ignore these signs, and focus narrowly on your goals, you may reach a physical and psychological exhaustion, which will exacerbate your vulnerability to traumatic symptoms.

6

The News Media's Role in Transmitting or Healing Trauma

As the media reports global tragedies, war, and violence on a daily basis, it is, in fact, exposing us to these traumas every day. By the same token, the media can have a central role in educating the public about trauma, its costs to individuals and society, as well as its impact on political policy, both nationally and internationally. Reporters can thus be ideally and uniquely positioned to help us recognize the long-term impact of trauma on individuals and nations and to play a role in healing trauma domestically and globally.

The media can reduce the immediate impact of trauma and have far-reaching effects on the physical and mental health of the world because of its capacity to disseminate information to billions of people at the same time. It can play an influential role in minimizing the impact of trauma by raising political awareness. It is the only organization that can rapidly put trauma on the global agenda and increase awareness of solutions to heal it.

In order to effect that healing, we need to offer validation of suffering and international forums for handling grievances. We need to help with mediation teams well grounded in the knowledge of history and cross-cultural understanding. We need to introduce cutting-edge methods of trauma treatment that can be taught at mass levels. We need to face what was done as well as note the reasons why it was done. It is a monumental task that can only be accomplished with the help of a media well versed in trauma.

A safer and healthier world will emerge when trauma can be more fully understood in this context. Trauma specialists need to work hand in hand with the media to bring this awareness to the public, governments, and international bodies as they continue to explore trauma's impact on political events.

The media can be a force for positive change, but it can also be the means by which trauma is brought directly to our living rooms. For instance, trauma's hypnotic pull explains the public's drive for repetitive viewing and the media's repetitive showing of violent and tragic events. Audiences that gravitate to extreme programming, who are "glued to the tube," hypnotized repetitively by traumatic images, are quite vulnerable to the magnetism of secondhand trauma and, along with media professionals, can be caught in a collective traumatic vortex.

Furthermore, the media can also unwittingly support the transmission of trauma by providing a forum for copycat crimes, by sensationalizing traumatic news, and by falling victim to manipulation by unscrupulous governments and government-controlled news agencies, themselves caught up in the trauma vortex.

THE TRAUMA VORTEX INFILTRATES OUR COLLECTIVE CONSCIOUSNESS

Traumatic events occur regularly in every corner of the world and are reported by the international press. These continual transmissions of tragedy represent the trauma vortex operating at the collective level. We have become simultaneously mesmerized and anesthetized by violence and tragedy. For instance, the world was unable to tear itself away from on-the-spot coverage of the car wreck that killed Princess Diana or the plane crash that killed John Kennedy Jr. The death of Princess Diana was a positive example of the world community grieving in unison for a life snuffed out at the height of its power and youth. Kennedy's plane crash represented the same grief, but the fact that the crash was replayed repeatedly left thousands of people scared to fly.

The numbing to violence has taken over some of our youth. Violence has always been with us, as well as the insensitivity to violence. However, more and more young people are getting caught in the trauma vortex, and at younger and younger ages.

Sis Levin, the wife of former CNN Bureau Chief in Lebanon Jerry Levin, told me the story that left an indelible image of her Lebanon experience: "let me tell what I saw. I turned the corner and on the curb was a little five-year-old with a pacifier in his mouth and a weapon on his lap. They are killing each other and killing adults too. They have been so brutalized, like in a whirlpool." Consider the response of David Cash, a high school boy whose friend Jeremy Strohmeyer murdered and raped seven-year-old Sherrice Iverson in Las Vegas. He claimed that he did not stop his friend because the crime was none of his business and he "did not know the girl." He even became popular with some of the girls in his school because of his involvement at the scene of the crime and for having been interviewed on television. It is also true that others regarded him as a monster and protested against him enrolling in their college.

During the Gulf War many people were captivated by the horrifying images shown repetitively on television, even though they knew themselves to be deeply troubled and depressed by them. During the 1992 Los Angeles riots, a syndicated columnist, who wants to remain anonymous, noted that, "the incessant news coverage kept people glued to the screen. It might have even unwittingly encouraged some people to participate in the looting." The capacity to think and reflect, to empathize and take action, is replaced by a hypnotic sensory overstimulation, leading to an increased tolerance to hyperarousal—that rush of adrenaline in response to threat or excitation. Members of the media and the audience can get quite caught up in the ongoing cycle of this secondhand trauma vortex.

> Unresolved trauma breeds the "repetition compulsion" in the hopes of finally mastering trauma the next time around.

The repeated viewing of graphic reports sets up a similar unconscious pattern: "If I watch tragic stories long enough, I can learn to overcome my fear of them." What happens instead, however, is that we develop a sensory tolerance for the gruesome. Both the media and the public find themselves locked in a whirlpool of overstimulation, resulting in obsessively observing, reporting, watching, and talking about the horrible. This keeps us fixated on the traumatic wound.

Right after September 11, I gave a three-page article I had written on Emotional First Aid to Steve, a friend who was helping me repair my printer. When I asked him the next day whether it helped him or not, he put it this way: "The most important thing I learned is that when I was watching the news nonstop for days, it was like I was eating these traumatic images, I was feeding myself with trauma, I was growing a belly of trauma."

THE COPYCAT PHENOMENON

The copycat phenomenon refers to individuals acting out or "copying" a reported event. There are compelling examples of the effect of copycat phenomenon in our own media history. We are reminded of beneficial examples from as far back as a decades-old episode of *Happy Days*. The teenage role model, Fonzi, applied for a library card, and the following week thousands of young students got their own cards. Oprah Winfrey interviews a woman who reveals her sexual abuse as a child for the first time, and hundreds of women dial for a therapist to process traumas they'd hidden for their whole lives. When Oprah was doing her Book Club, she would talk to her audience about how a book revolutionized her life, and the book would become an instant bestseller.

After September 11, the intense coverage of the courage of firemen and policemen risking their lives to save the people in their community encouraged hundreds of young people to want to join the departments. Applications to the law-enforcement agencies—city police, FBI, CIA—and city fire departments were at an all-time high, possibly the highest in history. Many more people than usual dressed up as firefighters and policemen for Halloween instead of traditional scary garb—costume shops reported that they were running out of such costumes because the demand was so large. Also, after a call for blood donations in New York and other cities, so many people all over the nation rushed to donate blood that there were waiting lists and lines at donation centers. The public responds each time to calls of help in dire circumstances.

Many organizations attempt to create a positive copycat phenomenon effect by doing social marketing, pushing and promoting stories with social issues. Mediascope, a fair-minded and friendly media watchdog organization in Los Angeles, reported the example of an episode of *Hey Arnold*, a children's cartoon, which demonstrated the Heimlich maneuver. A child saw the show and performed the maneuver on a friend who was choking. Hundreds of people signed up for CPR classes after *Baywatch* showed scenes of people performing CPR and saving lives. In Tanzania, a show was created to promote ethnic tolerance and diversity; it was reported in *USA Today* that children became less prejudiced as a result of the show. A 1997 study done in conjunction with the TV medical drama *ER* surveyed a number of people on the effect the show had on them. Nearly one-third of those surveyed said they got information from the show that helped them make choices about their own family's health care.

Alternately, the tragic side of the copycat coin was illustrated right after the news coverage of the Littleton tragedy. Immediately following the rampage at Columbine High School, one thousand bomb scares in Mexico and hundreds of copycat threats, along with some actual occurrences, popped up around the United States and Mexico. The same held true after the first anthrax letters were discovered in October 2001.

When the media is blamed for the results of a copycat crime, it may rightly become defensive, fearing legislation, legal sanctions, or a limiting of freedom of speech. With a few exceptions, confrontations and counterattacks rather than communication and problem solving have been the norm between the media and its accusers. Responsibility needs to be shared by all: the media, the government, and the general public.

Consider how the presentation of events can inspire the copycat phenomenon. CNN shows excited and angry young Pakistanis joining the Taliban in Afghanistan. They also show a demonstration of a few thousands Pakistanis against their government for its cooperation with the America. These images typically increase a sense of fear and anxiety in the West and exacerbate the trauma vortex. Just as seriously, they may also incite many Muslim young men, offering excitement and a *raison d'être* they might not find elsewhere in their lives.

One possible way to counteract these images may be to put their numbers in perspective and show in the same report or soon thereafter the millions of Pakistanis who do not think joining the Taliban's war is a good idea. Programming can include calls of religious leaders cautioning their youth against this influence, or mention casualties that have already occurred amongst the Taliban and their allies.

The media has been seriously concerned with the copycat phenomenon and is attempting to address this issue. Several media organizations have been preoccupied with the influence of media on the public. However, it seems that this preoccupation does not always translate into policy. This may be an area where collaboration with psychologists and trauma specialists is of crucial importance. For example, after September 11, the media set up a forum for intelligent discourse, analyzing all the elements involved in current terrorist activity: the ideological reasons for it, the cross-cultural nature of the conflict, the effect of our responses, and the public's reaction. It helped the public by televising dialogs on the possible triggers surrounding the attack. Adding the angles of trauma and mass psychology as influences on the copycat phenomenon can shed further light and help reinforce the healing vortex.

It is particularly crucial now to be aware of the copycat phenomenon on the international scene regarding the behavior of groups and nations during the current political events. The searing images of the collapsing Twin Towers repeated over and over and the later alerts of ongoing threat of anthrax and biochemical terrorism brought home to Americans feelings of helplessness and deep worry that their country had been weakened. However, these repeated images can drive the picture of a vulnerable America deeper into their adversaries' psyches and inspire more terrorism as it reinforces the terrorists' sense of power. We have already seen the media utilize discernment regarding how adversaries and the public may react to certain data and the way it is delivered. Cooperation with our government's request to limit bin Laden's airtime was well received. Is there more that can be done?

As of this writing, there is no clear picture of the impact of the copycat phenomenon on negative situations. Therefore, it behooves us to look carefully at all the issues that may negatively affect an already aggravated public. It is crucial to engage our best minds, including media trendsetters, in a comprehensive analysis of the phenomenon, so that more destruction does not take place. Transcending politics, the media could engage in being a healing force in the world by addressing the impact of trauma on society as well as on international politics. At the same time, it might be in the position to make a judgment call on the situation by engaging in constructive countering of the trauma vortex and emphasizing the healing vortex.

A recent and hopeful example of collaboration is the London Conference, organized by the BBC World Service in partnership with the Dart Center for Journalism and Trauma. More than sixty journalists, psychotherapists, editors, and journalism educators from Britain and the U.S. met to discuss new ways to support journalists who report on traumatic events. It is the beginning of a more elaborate dialogue to better serve the public.

THE ACCUSATION OF SENSATIONALISM

There are many pressures on television news to emphasize violence in their coverage. "If it bleeds, it leads," said Paul Klite of Rocky Mountain Media Watch. Local TV carries little that affects its community, while "a whole range of important news is choked off," he said. His organization examined the content of local television news for a "snapshot" four years in a row. Its most recent report, in August 1998, said coverage of violent events averaged just over 40 percent of all the news on one specific day on 102 stations in 52 metropolitan areas. Klite called it "a toxic diet" of news.

"It's purely economic," explains Emmy-winning KTLA news producer Dave Saldana. "Especially in a competitive market, stations that break from 'If it bleeds, it leads' tend to suffer in the ratings, so they don't stick with it. The market is what drives the coverage." Those pressures are real in a metropolitan area as large as Los Angeles, where up to 15 million people may be watching newscasts. "The competition is tough," Linda Alvarez of Los Angeles' KCBS explained in *Freedom Forum,* a non-partisan organ dedicated to free press. "Seven TV stations and thirty hours of [news] product every day."

"Common to all stations, we want to be first with the story," said John Sears, News Director of KPTV in Portland, Oregon. "We want to distinguish ourselves from 100 channels." Modern ratings services, which provide the data on which television stations base advertising rates, are so sophisticated that executives can know how their station fared competitively in any fifteen-minute increment, according to Sears. "Ratings are significant. They're like an overnight report card and influence how news is covered," adds Alvarez.

Moderator Robert MacNeil, a retired broadcast journalist, said critics of local TV news characterized it as "body bags at eleven" because of its high crime content. And yet, he noted, 80 million Americans watch local news every day, an audience greater than national newscasts attract.

But there are mitigating forces. Angie Kucharski, news director of WBNS-TV in Columbus, Ohio, called surveys like those conducted by Paul Klite's organization blanket generalizations. "It may be a story of a man who saved someone after an accident—is that violence?" she asked. Angela Davis, a reporter for WFAA-TV in Dallas, conceded in *Freedom Forum* that "mayhem, fluff, sex and violence" do get into newscasts but "we are also going to tell you what the mayor said today and what happened in the school district."

Does television news show the most graphic footage available? The Radio and Television News Directors' newsletter, *Communicator,* notes, "It's becoming standard fare for daytime and even late-night newscasts to air verbal warnings before showing graphic film or a foul-mouthed source. Warning viewers that graphic content is on its way is a courtesy to parents whose children may be watching the news," says Michael Espinoza, news director for KFSN-TV in Fresno, California. "Parents don't necessarily expect us to show somebody getting shot on the news," he says, "so we let them know."

A 1993 study by the Times Mirror Center for the People & The Press revealed that more than half of parents with children between the ages of eight and thirteen say their kids watch the news either regularly or sometimes. And six out of ten parents in the survey said they worry "a great deal" or "a fair amount" that their children might be disturbed by what they see on TV newscasts. In fact, more than half of the parents in the study said they have either changed the channel or turned the TV set off during a newscast that aired something—usually sex- or violence-related—that they did not want their children to see.

In a February 1998 article in *Communicator* entitled, "What You're About to See Is Shocking," Dan Amundson, Research Director for the Center for Media and Public Affairs in Washington, D.C., says most stories can survive without the show-everything shots. "Discussing it isn't as dramatic as something with a lot of visual images," he admits. "But there's no reason to shock [viewers]. A verbal description of [the news event] doesn't have the shock value."

"It seems to me that we make money out of exploiting suffering. We package trauma," said Gibbs when I interviewed her. Though she thought the media would be reluctant to change, she also acknowledged that it had often recognized and mirrored necessary changes in society. Certainly, after September 11, both news and entertainment media became more aware of trauma and its impact, and much more open to the possibility of playing a crucial role in the recovery process.

The traumatic shock of the attacks is a clear example of how widely and immediately trauma can affect hundred of millions at once. This traumatic shock seemed on the verge of turning into a trauma vortex that could well engulf America and the whole Islamic world and consequently the planet. Instinctively, the American and the international media responded well. If the media had focused only on the Americans' angry response, they would not have helped the public place it in a larger perspective of further stages of resolution. The anger phase could have spread like a virus and could have manifested with angry policymakers, supported by an enraged public, determining premature or inflexible military actions. It could have spun further into a larger trauma vortex.

As it is, the media acted responsibly and addressed the different quandaries reflected in the population. It focused on anger, but also on the determination and courage of the American public, its soul searching, and its intent to protect civil liberties and religious freedom, including the well being of its Muslim population. It is apparent that the media is the entity that can carry to the public a comprehensive understanding of the different stages of traumatic responses and how to cope with trauma.

THE DANGERS OF SUBTLE MANIPULATION

During the Gulf War, Iraqis watched CNN reports to get information on the fate of their own country. Today, many countries have their own well-organized media. The governments of some countries have been and are presently using the press for indoctrination and the promotion of a spirit of war. The international media can be an unwitting participant even with "objective" reporting when indoctrination media is unidentified and is reported as news only, when there is only one source, or when the journalist does not have enough background history. There is a beginning awareness in the field that the press can be subtly manipulated to further the promotion of conflict.

A round table took place at Radio Free Europe/Radio Liberty, in Prague, on October 16, 2002, on the topic of the media's role in covering modern-day war and conflict and the changing roles and challenges for journalists. "Reporting about war is a complicated task," said Ricchiardi, a senior writer with American Journalism Review, "It is easy to take one side on an issue, but a good journalist must strive for accuracy and balance." Indeed, it becomes crucial to be keenly conscious of the total impact of whatever is reported. Today, nothing falls on objective ears. For that matter, journalists need to become schooled on how they, themselves, can personally be pulled by the trauma vortex of the people they are covering. It is important that they realize how subtle the pull can be and how it can affect their accuracy and capacity to judge the situation. The awareness of the pull of one trauma vortex appealing to us more than another may help the international community not be caught in the warring countries' trauma vortexes, but instead warn and put pressure on these countries where indoctrination is taking place and help their media people be free from serving destructive state policies.

> Nations in conflict naturally escalate the trauma vortex just by reporting all the tragedies and sufferings of war. But the damage is manifold when they continuously run traumatic images on television from the past or the present. And even more damaging and trauma-vortex inspired are fabrications of traumatic images.

Recently, for example, Arab television showed fabrications of traumatizing images that incited their viewers to more hatred—scenarios of Israeli soldiers raping little Arab girls or throwing poison-laced candies to Arab youngsters. The Taliban showed Americans throwing food packages laced with poison to Afghani children. Some Arab leaders exacerbate the trauma of their people to encourage a more fundamentalist outlook. We need to be aware of the possibility that these leaders themselves are driven by unresolved previous personal, cultural, or national traumas.

As conscious misinformation can be an incredible political weapon—that is being used more articulately than ever before—it becomes of essence for the media to be on guard and take more time to investigate the veracity of what is being brought to it. It also becomes necessary to understand the psychological manipulations that all human beings can become prey to, when they are prey to the trauma vortex.

On the other hand, the following is an example of positive use of the media that can have political impact if much more of these efforts were made. In the thickest of the Israeli military operations in Palestinian territories, in which each side was totally convinced of its own victim status and the monstrosity of the actions and intentions of their enemy, an American network showed a story of generosity and gratitude crossing enemy lines. The family of an Israeli suicide-bombing victim donated his organs to the hospital where one of the organs was transplanted into a Palestinian woman to save her life. The report showed her grateful children visiting the mourning Israeli family and "sitting shiva," mourning with them. This is the kind of journalistic effort that encourages the healing vortex.

THE MEDIA'S CHALLENGE

Clearly, the media has the power to stir up passions. It has long been used as a vehicle to mobilize people around an issue, be it the German media rallying Nazi sympathizers to the Third Reich, American newsreels rallying concerned citizens during World War II, or Al Jazeera rallying Muslims around the world. The media is one of the most powerful forces in shaping the world in the twenty-first century. It is more influential than ever as information is now instantly accessible to the entire world, seven days a week, twenty-four hours a day. The capacity to televise anything live from anywhere has changed the impact of information. Critical though this change may be, we may not have slowed down long enough to analyze this shift or evaluate its effects.

The media's challenge in the new millennium is as follows: If coverage of trauma helps to "normalize" violence, then coverage of our collective healing capacity could normalize harmony. Members of the press can and increasingly do take on leadership roles that support the best values of our society in unprecedented ways. The media determines what the general public will see, and it knows how to use the power of suggestion. It can reflect society in ways that foster well being by covering tragic events in the context of the healing vortex. For instance, when the press focused on people in New York helping each other instead of dwelling on looters, it demonstrated its capacity to be guided by the healing vortex. If this becomes a voluntary and more widespread policy, such a visionary role can create meaningful bonding and loyalty between the media and its public, and more crucially, this role can help interrupt the cycle of violence and trauma.

The media can further counteract the powerfully magnetic pull of the trauma vortex by consciously tipping or evening out the scale toward the coverage of positive and uplifting events. Collaboration with trauma specialists to develop models and test strategies on how to inform the public with as little secondhand traumatization as possible can yield extraordinary results. Visionary professionals in both fields can work together on transforming the media's impact on society in relationship to trauma.

If the threat of a Third World War is looming, much of it might be fought through the media. This implies an involvement that was not part of the media's original mission—to report objectively and to inform the public about world events. Reporters in Bosnia took it upon themselves to tell the stories of children and women's suffering and influenced the intervention of Europe and the United States. Today, reporters are being called to testify in international courts about war horrors they witnessed. The media's task is constantly changing; their influence on history is stronger than ever.

As the media's role expands, their responsibility must expand with it intrinsically. The awareness of the trauma vortex must become pervasive as their role to put trauma and its healing on the global agenda can change how society operates.

The media's added task might very well become to consciously counterbalance the effect of unwittingly amplifying the trauma vortex just from covering it. Furthermore, the media needs to be conscious that its mere presence as an observer changes the object observed. This is in accordance with Neil Bohr's theory that research scientists affect the object of their research just in their mere observing of it. International media needs to also be aware of the influence of state-run media in non-democratic countries exacerbating and inciting trauma.

In explosive areas such as the Middle East, other efforts could include recognizing cultural traumas and validating grievances without indulging in the role of the victim. Specialists in trauma, the psychology of human behavior, mediation, and cross-cultural awareness can clearly be of help. This type of collaboration may change how things have been done until now.

7

THE HEALING VORTEX

As the media better understands trauma-based dynamics, it can take action to interrupt the cycles of trauma related to news coverage. There are constructive ways in which it can truly serve the public. When violence is shown as a public health issue, audiences can emerge better educated, enlightened about their pain and empowered. Some practical ways the media can do this are:

- Explain to the public that they need to keep reporting the tragedy so that viewers can tune in at all times.

- Explain the pull the trauma vortex has on especially sensitive people and how it keeps them glued to the tube, ingesting the same traumatic images over and over, "creating a belly of trauma."

- Recommend to their viewers to get the information offered and then turn to other activities that will calm them.

- Suggest that viewers tune in later for further news and resources.

In a broader context, media organizations can sponsor well-funded and rigorous research on the press's impact on society. They can take a leading role in hosting public discourse on values and policies. They already hold politicians and public institutions responsible for demonstrating integrity in their public functions.

Developing their watchdog organizations is very useful, but also assures that the findings translate into ongoing policy. An excellent example of such organizations include the recently created Norman Lear Center, whose mission is to study the impact of the media on society's values. The Creative Coalition—a nonprofit organization of arts and entertainment community members advocating important social and political issues in the area of the First Amendment and public education—is another viable resource.

Mark Brayne, BBC foreign correspondent and psychotherapist, argues that correspondents must pay attention to their own experience as they reflect to their listeners an image of their own world. Only if they do it with awareness and authenticity can their reporting resonate as authentic and reliable. He goes on to point out where the media needs to change its focus. When reporters deny the emotional and spiritual dimension of their experience and distort the world, it may make for striking and eye-catching headlines, but the results can be "uninteresting and even irresponsible," he maintains.

To his journalistic talents, Brayne brings a therapist's understanding to the importance of making connections, the destructiveness of labels, and the supreme benefit that comes from understanding and from witnessing the emotional dimension of events with compassionate neutrality. "News which reports trauma and violence, yes—the First Act, as it were, of the drama," he explains. "But emotionally intelligent news, which also follows through to Act Two—to healing and change. It may be about healthier journalists. It is also about better journalism."

OUR HOPE: THE HEALING VORTEX

What is most energizing about trauma, paradoxically, is that its healing is transformative for the individual as well as for society.

Knowing how unresolved trauma engenders pessimism, cynicism, despair, and paralysis of the will, on one hand, and desperate and uncontrolled acting out, on the other, we can understand how healing opens the door to hope, optimism, and the desire for creative action.

The capacity to heal is always present and accounts for humanity's remarkable resiliency. Given the amount of traumatization, neglect, and strife in the world, it is amazing that people do so well. But sometimes innate healing does get blocked when unresolved traumas overwhelm the innate capacity to heal and trigger a downward spiral. We can restore the healing capacity by respecting and working with our physiological and neurological patterns. In the last several years, the scientific community has developed a number of methods to release and master traumatic events, memories, and patterns (many of these will be described in greater detail in Chapter 11). With these proactive interventions, trauma's momentum can be reversed and the equally dynamic upward cycle generated. Furthermore, these techniques can help develop resiliency from trauma, a task crucially needed in the immediate future.

The only way to reduce our individual and societal traumatic legacies is to transform them. Levine's "healing vortex" is a transformative process. Immediately after a traumatic event, the swirling motion of the trauma vortex is directly counteracted by its opposite, the motion of the healing vortex. But because our bodies and psyches have been overwhelmed with so much collective trauma this last century, we need more awareness to help activate the innate healing vortex. One way to remedy this problem is to learn how to reconnect to our animal instincts and reconnect with the body/mind. We can do so by bringing our full awareness to the sensations in our body and allowing the organic process to take place, using our intelligence in a compassionate way.

Witnessing without judgment what's going on within our senses and at the emotional, thinking, and behavioral levels allows our body to discharge the traumatic energy and return to the natural cycles of trauma and healing, to our natural capacity to cope with tragedy. When we regain this balance, both personally and collectively, we can hope of bringing up our children in a safer world.

The mass media has enabled change to occur in the way people in many nations think and act regarding race issues, gender differences, and the environment, to name a few. In the United States, great educational strides have been taken against drunk driving, unprotected sex, and smoking. Society has a huge reservoir of healing efforts with which the media can and does collaborate to make information available.

THE ROLE OF THE MEDIA IN HEALING TRAUMA

In regards to trauma, the fundamental question is this: can people be offered the necessary information and the available resources to deal with the trauma and violence that the media report on so that they are not left feeling scared, powerless, or numb? Two issues come together here: what is reported and how is it reported? As one journalist told me, "The trend is that more bad news is presented than good news, and the shock stories are front-loaded in the news hour. A life taken is believed to be more attention-grabbing than a life saved." This is a diagnosis that does not take into account what we know about trauma and about the pull of the trauma vortex. Without a doubt, a life taken is traumatizing and will naturally be attention-grabbing. That is specifically the nature of trauma—to grab all of our focus and energy; it is certainly the nature of trauma that "whatever kills the most gets the front page."

Nevertheless, this problem of "bad news" versus "good news" can be resolved fairly easily, within the context of understanding trauma. The effect of traumatic stories can be counteracted by giving attention to the consequences of the events and the opportunities for healing available to the survivors. It is possible that seemingly overwhelming obstacles for media people truly interested in helping the public address traumatic issues in a constructive manner might not be as daunting as first thought. Such an approach might actually capture a larger audience, "run more ink," and open opportunities for human-interest stories. An example of a media group that in fact chooses to run life-affirming stories can be found at www.positivepress.com, which culls its stories from many sources.

It can be just as lucrative for the media to address these wider issues of trauma. There can be power and profit in this change. This was true when the news became a business. It can also be true when the media becomes an educator on trauma. Serving the healing vortex does not have to equal losing profits. The material of human interest related to tragedy and violence is inexhaustible. And as journalist Liisa Hyvarinem, also a Dart fellow, expressed, "People like to read good news." Clearly, this awareness must translate into changes at the editorial and management level.

We Need to Normalize Trauma, not Violence

I am not suggesting that the media minimize covering the tragic, which would only serve to keep the public ill-informed, but rather to develop a more trauma-informed and complete level of presentation. Visual pictures of reality are a good way for us to know the truth. If on-the-spot coverage had been available during World

War II and scenes of the concentration camps could have been witnessed—however traumatizing that would have been—public awareness and pressure might have hastened their demise. Earlier images of the rapes and killings of women by the Serbs might have sped American military intervention. The objective is not to disband coverage. The premise, rather, is that coverage of the tragic and violent might have gone overboard because of the magnetic pull of the trauma vortex. It needs to be balanced by a conscious attempt at covering the healing vortex, skillfully presenting the healing aspect side of the traumatic events covered and refocusing on a higher percentage of non-traumatic events.

The public needs to know and understand the varied manifestations of trauma. The September 11 attacks have turned trauma into a household topic. As a result, trauma lost some of its stigma. But there will be many distortions as the word morphs into a catchall that is poorly understood. For example, we do not all have to be traumatized because we witness or live through traumatic events. Most of us learn to cope on our own, and our lives won't have to be "changed forever." But we may also need to overcome the misconceptions and the ignorance regarding the manifestations of psychological trauma and neutralize the stigma it may still carry for too many people, especially concerning events that are not recognized as traumatic.

Retired reporter Akila Gibbs captures the elusive nature of trauma perfectly:

> We need to understand what trauma is. We often don't even want to remember an event, so we tend to oversimplify it. Sometimes we don't even know that we are taking it in. We know that something is unpleasant, we know it feels bad, but we don't know it is actually traumatizing, and that it has

a powerful and extensive impact on us. People are so used to hearing the word "abuse" that they forget it is a major injury with lasting effects. We practice the art of avoidance by taking a pill, going on vacation, buying a new house, and we think all is well.

Specific Ways the News Media Can Help

When the media develops an accurate understanding of the patterns of traumatization and the pull of the trauma vortex, it can recognize that an emphasis on the violent, the abnormal, and the tragic is an understandable and dangerous manifestation of the trauma vortex. It will recognize the trauma vortex's relentless pull in conflicts and war between tribes and nations and how it affects both the selection and the delivery of news. Then the media will add to its coverage the awareness of this pull. It will add the attempts of people and institutions to work with the healing vortex. This new perspective can foster an organic and balanced shift in the media's coverage of events and help people recover faster.

There are simple but specific changes in news coverage that have the power to bring about a healthier society. This can be done by:

1. Inserting healing images along with the coverage of traumatic events.

"Find ways people are helping, including acts of kindness, and report on them throughout the recovery process. This may provide hope for the community," advise Joe Hight and Frank Smyth in "Tragedies and Journalist: A Guide for More Effective Coverage." Imagine a five-year-old who becomes scared while watching the endlessly repetitive images of a Los Angeles fire on the news. He starts having nightmares and asks his mother, "Why didn't the fire stop?" Televising the firefighters' attempts at controlling the fire, talking about its containment, and showing that people in the area are safe can make a big difference to this five-year-old.

2. Becoming aware of the "tunnel vision" of a trauma-saturated perspective.

With an understanding of the trauma vortex and its counter-vortex, the media has the opportunity to balance the effects of tragic stories. A heavy focus on negative news unwittingly reinforces people's fears or tendency toward violence. At any given moment, there are endless examples of violence and catastrophes to cover, as well as endless examples of courage and resiliency. There is the need to assess whether a news item is likely to add to the well being of society or worsen it. A choice of what to cover is taking place anyhow. Questions to ask: Which events should we choose? How many of each kind? What are the criteria? Why do we choose them? Does the public truly benefit from this piece of news rather than this other one? How would we cover it? Does it serve the trauma or the healing vortex? Are ratings a sufficient indicator of the public opinion?

3. Recognizing and analyzing the copycat phenomenon with the help of psychological researchers.

Working in tandem with the therapeutic community on how to present tragedies in a manner that does not feed the copycat phenomenon might have helped in the aftermath of Columbine, for instance. (This may include the disclosing of neither the identity of the perpetrators, nor giving air-time to their distorted messages.) A few years ago, local TV reporting of teen suicides directly caused numerous copycat suicides of impressionable teenagers. "I know how to get my picture on TV, too," was part of the reasoning. Due to the research done regarding these "cluster suicides," television stations, in general, no longer cover teenage suicides.

4. Warning viewers of upcoming disturbing images.

Besides children, older people, and many sensitive women do not turn on the TV for fear of seeing traumatic images. One suggestion is to take the bad news in small doses and immediately thereafter engage in an activity that helps them calm down, relax, and feel stronger. In Somatic Experiencing and other techniques, these types of activity are called resources. Several radio stations warned their viewers about the hazards of watching too much TV on the anniversary date of the September 11 attacks.

5. Blacking out gory details such as remains or disposal of bodies, visual evidence of brutality, and instruments of torture.

We routinely bleep sexual and curse words. We could readily obscure gory details once we understand how disturbing their effects are on children and sensitive adults. Although the collapsing towers of the World Trade Center of September 11 were shown over and over, as well as the images of the falling bodies, the media restrained itself from repeatedly showing the gruesome images at Ground Zero.

6. Avoiding incessant coverage of events involving violence or tragedy and repetitive showing of disturbing images.

The repetition drives the image deep into the psyche and puts people at risk for flashbacks and obsessive thoughts.

7. Warning viewers that incessant watching could be disturbing.

For instance, one station decided not to cover the Littleton tragedy until eleven o'clock at night to mute its impact on children. That is an example of sensitive, responsible, and empathic coverage. In another incident of live coverage of a stand-off between the police and a runaway car in which the pursued man shot himself, some news stations, shaken by what happened, decided to allow a few second intervals between the live shooting of a scene and its transmission for fear that children might be exposed again to unexpected live tragedy. Consider yet this situation: a four-year-old boy thought that kids were shooting other children in many schools, not understanding that his station was rerunning the same tape of a school shooting. It is true that it is up to the parents to choose what their children watch, but the first evening news is broadcast during family hour, and the media and the public need to be made more aware of children's vulnerability.

8. *Informing viewers of the help available while the tragic events are being reported.*

Run help line and trauma phone numbers on the screen or show how people are being helped, as sometimes occurs.

9. *Recognizing that the observer of any event becomes part of the event (Niels Bohr's theory).*

As observers of society, the media influence events just by the act of observing, and more significantly, the act of reporting. We all need to reassess what we think of as objectivity.

10. *Avoiding reporting speculation and rumors that can cause anxiety and provoke erroneous conclusions that are much harder to dispel.*

The pressure is great to deliver cutting-edge news. Clearly many media members have made real efforts in this regard.

11. *Understanding the vulnerability of victims and avoiding unnecessary broadcasting of details that embarrass, humiliate, or hurt victims of crime.*

Victims' lack of privacy destabilizes the privacy and sense of safety of all of us. Do we really have the right to know everything about a public personality, even while this piece of information adds nothing to our lives but creates havoc in that person's life? The Ted Koppel *Nightline* show on ABC, on January 15, 2002, pointed a reflective finger at the press for revealing the drug problem of the Prince Henry of England, even though public figures are held to different standards. Media must be conscious of making stories about victims as personable and humane as possible.

12. Recognizing how coverage affects the reaction of the public.

The style of coverage will impact how the public will receive and react to traumatic news. "The news—thoroughly reported, verified, placed in context—should never inspire irrational fears. The information we provide, and the tone of its delivery, will go a long way to mobilize the public toward reasonable action, minimize panic, and offer some hope for the future," said Roy Peter Clark in his article "Tragedy & Journalists: A Guide for More Effective Coverage," published by the Dart Center for Journalism and Trauma.

13. Checking the tendency to look for spins on coverage
*   to keep a story in the news.*

There may be a tendency to keep milking a story by presenting new angles and interpretations—in lieu of any new information.

14. De-emphasizing the cult of celebrities, especially
*   the ones who act out or commit crimes or violence.*

Too many celebrities and political figures are left unscathed despite their often less than admirable behavior, serving as examples of impunity to impressionable youth.

15. Withholding the identity of perpetrators to deprive them
*   of their "fifteen minutes of fame."*

Too often, perpetrators are allowed to pronounce their destructive messages, thus encouraging copycat behavior. The public is ready for more upbeat reporting; witness its positive response to the firemen in New York as heroes.

16. Speculation about political conflicts.

Errors are almost inevitable, as journalists often need to write their reports before all the information is available, basing their writing on hearsay. However, in an age where the media is used as a political weapon and false claims with serious results can be easily made, the effects of speculation can be extremely damaging. When proven false, speculations need to be retracted, more often than they are. They need to be retracted immediately and given coverage proportionally to their impact. Speculation is a normal hazard in the reporting business. Both the media and the public need to acknowledge it. The media needs to take responsibility to openly correct the errors that arise from speculation, allowing it to become a matter of fact that will inspire trust in the media.

17. Covering political and military conflicts, humanizing each side, and describing the life and experience of the people from both sides.

The media can show the woundedness, the pain, and the suffering of both sides and show the similarities in their humanity. In trauma and war, people lose track of the humanity of the other and urgently need to be reminded of it.

18. Writing about war atrocities within the context of trauma, its impact on people, and on the distortion of their worldview.

The media can report on war atrocities from a trauma framework, including the underlying psychological traumas of the populations involved, the effect of those traumas on those populations, and their ensuing acting out. In doing so, the media may, by "normalizing" the actions as resulting from trauma and not from "pure evil," permit the parties in conflict to get enough validation of their pain to be able to understand and accept the distortions in their own thinking and move out of the trauma vortex.

19. *Keeping an "objective" eye on the beliefs, ideologies,*
   and worldviews of warring parties.

Collective trauma engages entire populations in viewing the "other" as dangerous. By not buying into one ideology over another, the media can encourage groups to look at their suffering, develop self-awareness, and engage in self-examination.

BEYOND "IF IT BLEEDS, IT LEADS"

The media doesn't stand to lose by adding a dimension of comprehensive information about trauma, and it will win, in return, particularly now, the gratefulness of its viewers. Indeed, humanity has been known for both meeting challenge and embracing spirit. Just as we have always been fascinated with tragedy, we are also drawn to courage, thirsty for spirituality, and aching for transformation. The public, though caught in the trauma vortex, is ready for healing too.

There are myriad examples of the media encouraging the development of the healing vortex in its presentation of news. Some examples from television are:

- At WNYT-TV in Albany, New York, News Director Paul Conti discouraged his staff from waiting for "body shots" on crime and disaster stories. He has also banned door-knocks with video rolling, and he is reticent to assign crews to stakeouts. He was the first to pull a crew from a stakeout at the Albany area home of relatives of Theodore Kaczynski, the accused Unabomber. (Oddly, Conti became the subject of a number of news stories as a result.)

- Many smaller-market news directors, including Tom Edwards at KTWO-TV in Casper, Wyoming, Jaime Cohen at WGGB-TV in Springfield, Massachusetts, and Marilyn Buerkle at WBOC-TV, in Salisbury, Maryland, aggressively pursue cause-and-solution sidebars with almost every major crime story. All said they shy away from airing gore.

- In Billings, Montana, John Stepanek of KTVQ-TV says his station is working to air more "proactive" stories about crime trends, crime prevention, and the burgeoning juvenile crime problem there while airing fewer pieces about routine crimes such as robberies and burglaries. He says these initiatives are designed to give viewers "a true picture of crime in the community."

- Chuck Ferrell, the assistant news director at WJRT-TV in Flint, Michigan, explains that his station carefully screens crime news for "trends and deeper significance. Just because there's been another shooting or homicide in Flint doesn't mean it's going to make the news that night," he says. WJRT is "a little ahead of the curve" on rational crime coverage because the station is sensitive to Flint's public image as a result of its unflattering portrayal in the 1989 film *Roger and Me*.

- As a result of viewer and staff comments about the superficial nature of crime coverage, WLKY-TV in Louisville, Kentucky, aired a thirty-two-part series entitled *Eye on Crime* in 1998 that took an encompassing look at the issue. The series continued that fall, says news director Michael Sipes. The station also has backed away from live shots of crime scenes—in part because a WLKY live van was fired upon at one such incident.

- As John Carr, Managing Editor at KCRA-TV in Sacramento, California, explains, "There has to be some strong, compelling reason to do a particular crime story, and the fact that you have a good piece of videotape is not a strong reason."

Furthermore, the media can actually affect and catalyze concrete positive change. One example is from an interview with documentary filmmaker Mandy Jacobsen, who addressed the cases of mass rapes in Bosnia in the *Columbia Journalism Review* in January 1993. Journalists covering these atrocities were actually able to effect political change regarding the rapes in this region and encourage intervention.

In response to the inquiry concerning why rape had become the focus of so much media attention and had been taken more seriously in this war than in others, Jacobsen recounts in her documentary: "Maggie O' Kane, a journalist from *The Guardian* who did a fantastic job in breaking a lot of the stories from eastern Bosnia about systematic rape, reckons that some of it had to do with the fact that 40 percent of people covering the war were women journalists, 'chicks in the zone' she calls them. If it weren't for the journalists, we wouldn't have been saved. The stories also impacted international policy because they've shamed politicians. And I find it fascinating that journalists are even being called to the Tribunal as expert witnesses. I'm sure journalists never thought of their roles like that in previous wars."

Another poignant example of media taking responsibility in the healing vortex is the story of journalist Donatella Lorch, who was compelled by her emotions to discard the attitude of the objective and detached observer and intervene, as reported in an interview with Joanmarie Kalter, a freelance journalist based in New Jersey. In 1999, Donatella Lorch was based in Albania, covering the stream of refugees from Kosovo. While on duty, she found a six-year-old boy ill with cancer and had him taken by helicopter to Italy for treatment. "That helps with all the stress," she says. "One producer told me to stop playing God. Another said, 'If playing God works, why not?'"

Good question. It is often expressed that effecting change positively was the original impetus for many in the media profession to enter into this field of work. There are many examples of media professionals assisting the public in various ways.

8

THE ENTERTAINMENT INDUSTRY'S ROLE IN TRANSMITTING OR HEALING TRAUMA

More than 3,000 laboratory experiments, field studies, and correlation studies have been conducted over the last 40 years on the effect of the entertainment industry on violence. These include 92 longitudinal studies spanning 22 years, two major meta-analyses, one examining 67 studies and over 30,000 subjects, and the other 230 studies and close to 100,000 subjects. Responding to the massive data, numerous parenting organizations, as well as health and government agencies, have accused the industry of being a major source of the violence that exists in our society.

Concurrently, the entertainment industry also focuses on trauma and violence as subjects for creativity. As Barbara Osborn, media literacy teacher, freelance journalist, and host of *Deadline LA*, on KPFK 90.7 FM in Los Angeles, explains, TV action series demonstrate an inclination for violence-driven stories. For example, "An episode of *Street Justice* promises: 'The brother of a suspected cop killer abducts Malloy in order to silence Beaudreaux, who is the only witness to the crime.' *On Star Trek: The Next Generation*, 'Geordi finds himself drawn romantically to a Starfleet lieutenant who is suspected of murder.' On a re-run of *Father Dowling Mysteries:*

'Someone takes a shot at Dowling and the culprit appears to be an angry ex-con Dowling helped send up the river on a murder rap.' TV and film plots begin with violence, and impending conflict continues to drive the story. The hero is never safe. Danger is always just around the corner. As the story unfolds, outbreaks of violence against people and property make sure that viewers stay in their seats."

Targeting a society of "channel surfers," the entertainment industry can inadvertently spread the impact of trauma in this way. However, unlike the tobacco industry, legislative action limiting the presentation of trauma and violence in the media is not a viable solution. The First Amendment protects freedom of speech. However, awareness of secondhand trauma can offer a powerful incentive for the entertainment industry to take some kind of action.

SOME BASIC FACTS ABOUT ENTERTAINMENT VIOLENCE

According to the Center for Media Education (CME), most children watch an average of three to four hours of TV per day, approximately twenty-eight hours each week. That translates into 1,500 hours in front of the TV each year. In fact, TV watching is the number one after school activity for six- to seventeen-year-olds. By the time the average child completes elementary school, he will have witnessed more than 100,000 acts of violence on television, including 8,000 murders. These numbers double to 200,000 acts of violence and 16,000 murders by the time he graduates from high school.

Lest one believe children's programming is a safe haven, research has shown that Saturday morning children's TV contains an average of twenty-six violent acts per hour compared to prime time during which five violent acts occur per hour. Before age eight, young children cannot uniformly discriminate between real life and fantasy entertainment and tend to learn by emulating. They quickly learn that violence is an acceptable solution to resolving even complex problems, particularly when the hero is the aggressor.

Media violence has a different effect on children than it does on adults. Children model behavior they see in the media. If kids don't see the consequences of violence, they learn that violence doesn't cause serious harm. When heroes use violence it sends a message that this is an appropriate way to respond to problems. If we were children, what lessons about the world might we learn from the programs we watch?

On the other hand, adults see much more violence in the media than actually exists in real life. Producers believe that they have to include extraordinary aggression in order to keep viewers interested. As a result, heavy TV viewers think that the world is more dangerous and violent than it actually is. This phenomenon is often called the "mean world" syndrome, and it is one that foments further anxiety, defensiveness, and in a few, even violence.

ARE THERE CONNECTIONS BETWEEN VIOLENCE IN ENTERTAINMENT AND VIOLENCE IN SOCIETY?

Academic critics, trauma experts, and media professionals have conflicting opinions on the subject. However, the average person believes there is a connection between the violence in the entertainment industry and the violence in society. According to media watchdog Mediascope, surveys have found that 82 percent of the American public considers movies too violent, 72 percent said that entertainment television has too much violence, and 57 percent think television news gives too much attention to stories about violent crime. Eighty-two percent of respondents feel that the amount of violence in American movies today is a serious problem for society, while 80 percent of Americans believe television violence is "harmful" to society. The number that thinks it is "very harmful" increased from 26 percent in 1983 to 47 percent in 1993.

A majority of Americans (53 percent) also believe that portrayals of violence in television, books, films, and newspaper stories make people more likely "to do something violent." In fact, 94 percent of adults support the notion that violence depicted in the media contributes to crime in America. In another study, 76 percent of respondents asserted that the depiction of violence in the media "numbs people to violence so that they're insensitive to it." Seventy-one percent responded that media depictions of violence tell people "that violence is fun and acceptable," while 75 percent believed that media violence inspires young people to violence.

Are these perceptions and beliefs based on fact?

More than one thousand studies including a Surgeon General's special report in 1972 and a National Institute of Mental Health report in 1982 do attest to a causal connection between media violence and aggressive behavior in some children. However, the good news is that it is not just any violence. Studies show that the more real-life the violence portrayed is, the greater the likelihood that it will be learned. The portrayal of violence as being justified (particularly by the "good guy") is the single most prevalent notion in American entertainment and the most powerfully reinforced one.

Alexandra Marks describes one of these studies in the April 17, 1998, issue of *The Christian Science Monitor*: "The simplicity of the experiment at the Minneapolis day-care center and the starkness of the results stunned the parents. When a class of two- to five-year-olds watched public television's big-hearted purple dinosaur, Barney, they sang along, marched along, held one another's hands, and laughed together. The next day, the same class watched the aggressive teenage avengers, *Power Rangers*. Within minutes, they were karate-chopping and high-kicking the air—and one another."

In "Trained to Kill," the August 10, 1998, cover story in *Christianity Today*, retired Lieutenant Colonel Dave Grossman, an author and leading expert on media violence and youth, reported on a definitive epidemiological study on the impact of TV violence previously published by the *Journal of the American Medical Association* on June 10, 1992. The research demonstrated what happened in numerous nations after television made its appearance as compared to nations and regions without TV.

Television was introduced for the first time in a Canadian town in 1973. A study showed that after exposure, there was a 160 percent increase in aggression, hitting, and biting in first- and second-graders while there was no change in behavior in the students of the two control communities. The communities being compared were demographically and ethnically identical; there was only one variable—the presence of television. In every nation, region, or city with television, there was an immediate explosion of violence on the playground, and within fifteen years, a doubling of the murder rate. Why fifteen years, you may ask? It seems that is how long it takes for the desensitization to violence of a three- to five-year-old to reach the "prime crime age." Could it be an accident that violence is exploding in the Muslim world fifteen years after TV and Western programming arrived? (Clearly variables other than the one of violence on television may have influenced this development.)

Given these shocking results, and even if TV is but one of the many influences on children's aggressive behavior, we must ask ourselves:

- Might a significant portion of the audience be already trau-matized and thus more vulnerable? Could it be that this audience is more predisposed to that influence, including people suffering from a broad range of unresolved traumatic events or conditions?

- Might children in general be the more vulnerable ones? Are young children particularly affected because they live in a state of imitation all the time and learn by role model?

- Is there something that the entertainment industry can do to present violence so as to minimize the chance of inciting aggression or trauma in the audience?

- Does the industry do anything to affect the audience's vulnerability to suggestions of violence or to fear?

- Can the industry do anything to lessen the audience's vulnerability to suggestions of violence?

Regardless of one's point of view, it will be helpful for the enter-tainment industry to learn what it can about trauma, violence, and media influence, and integrate this information into their vision of their role in society and into their creations. It is also in the public's interest for trauma research specialists to learn what media personnel have to deal with and engage them in a collab-orative effort, instead of using a critical and imposing tone.

HOW ENTERTAINMENT VIOLENCE INFLUENCES VIEWERS

There is general consensus in the scientific and public health fields that there are three primary harmful effects of viewing media vio-lence:

- Learning aggressive attitudes and behaviors;

- Emotional desensitization toward real world violence;

- Increased fear of being victimized by violence, resulting in self-protective behaviors, such as buying guns, and mistrust of others, which in turn might induce further violence.

These and other specific modes of behavior affecting viewers of entertainment violence were studied and analyzed in The National Television Violence Study (1996), a major investigation conducted by researchers at the Universities of North Carolina, Texas, California, and Wisconsin (facilitated and published by Mediascope). The study also identified that the risk of such effects occurring in viewers is influenced by how violence is depicted in the program. Once again, they found that if a character perceived as "good" is perpetrating the violence, viewers might acquire or learn that violent behavior; if the character is perceived as "evil," they might become fearful and more isolated.

The National Television Violence Study identified nine factors which, when viewed in context to the program, may contribute to positive or harmful effects on viewers.

- PERPETRATORS: Children were more likely to imitate behaviors learned from characters they liked, were fascinated by, or whom they thought were like them. Thus, watching a hero or superhero behave violently made them more likely to act aggressively than after watching a villain do so. The data on the effect of a violent good hero on children's aggressiveness, although counterintuitive, is revealing. Creating non-violent, good hero characters can guide the entertainment industry without much cost to creativity or output. To the contrary, it allows for a more original and complex ideas and character development.

- VICTIMS: If children perceived the victim of violence as attractive or like themselves, they were likely to experience heightened emotional involvement, anxiety, and fear.

- REASON: Violence shown as justified (the hero must eliminate the villain to save the world from harm) was more likely to encourage aggressive behavior. If the act is unjustified (a robber shoots a store clerk) the aggressive tendencies were reduced.

- WEAPONS: Surprisingly, even the presence of weapons alone was shown to activate aggressive thoughts and behaviors in viewers and to maybe influence the reading of neutral events as possibly threatening.

- PROLONGED EXPOSURE: Repeated entertainment violence could result in having a desensitizing and a numbing effect that inhibited sympathy and empathy. The overall effect of repeated entertainment violence could be the belief that violence was a viable way to solve problems, or to provoke un-involvement when violence happens in front of them.

- REALISM: Even though very young children do not always understand the difference between fantasy and reality, the more realistic a violent act was perceived to be, the more likely it was to elicit aggressive behavior.

- REWARDS AND PUNISHMENTS: It was self-evident that violence that is rewarded or that goes unpunished increases the likelihood of learning aggression in both children and adults. Violence that is punished decreases that risk.

- CONSEQUENCES: Visual depictions of pain and suffering have been shown to actually inhibit aggressive behavior in viewers. Aggression is increased when there are no consequences.

- HUMOR: Humor, when it is combined with violence, may trivialize it or decrease the audience's perception of its consequences.

In this discussion of violence in the entertainment industry, we must take into account what's called the *Japanese Conundrum.* The only country in the world with nearly as much entertainment violence as the United States is Japan. Yet Japanese society is far less violent than American society. If media violence contributes to real-life violence, why isn't Japanese society more affected? A 1981 study found that the nature of the portrayal of violence is different in Japan: there it is more realistic, and the consequences of violence are stressed by placing greater emphasis on physical suffering. Interestingly, in Japan the "bad guys" commit most of the violence, with the "good guys" suffering the consequences—the reverse of American programming. In this context, violence is seen as wrong, a villainous activity with real and painful consequences, rather than as justifiable.

WHAT ABOUT VIOLENT LYRICS IN SONGS?

According to the American Academy of Pediatrics (AAP), in *Impact of Music Lyrics and Rock Music Videos on Children and Youth,* the results of a survey of 2,760 fourteen- to sixteen-year-olds in ten different southeastern cities showed that teenagers listened to music an average of forty hours per week. However, "to date, no studies have documented a cause-and-effect relationship between sexually explicit or violent lyrics and adverse behavioral effects. A possible explanation for this lack of finding is that teenagers often do not know the lyrics or fully comprehend their meaning. For example, in one study, only 30 percent of teenagers knew the lyrics to their favorite songs, and their comprehension varied greatly. . . . Most teenagers tend to interpret their favorite songs as being about 'love, friendship, growing up, life's struggles, having fun, cars, religion, and other topics that relate to teenage life.'

However, for a small subgroup of teenagers, music preference may be highly significant. Numerous studies indicate that a preference for heavy metal music may be a significant marker for alienation, substance abuse, psychiatric disorders, suicide risk, sex-role stereotyping, or risk-taking behaviors during adolescence."

WHAT ABOUT VIDEO GAMES?

Retired Colonel David Grossman has sounded the alarm, after a recent speaking tour: parents must curb the use of the wildly popular genre of video games called "first person shooter," such as *Doom*, *Quake*, and *Duke Nukem*. In these games, the player sees through the gun sights of the character he plays as he moves through some sort of maze, gunning down various mutants, monsters, and other supernatural baddies. Grossman's argument is that in teaching the player to open fire reflexively, the games closely resemble techniques the military uses to break down a new recruit's inhibitions against killing, mainly through the use of human-shaped targets and repetition.

As Grossman emphatically puts it, "The military and law enforcement community have made killing a conditioned response. This has substantially raised the firing rate on the modern battlefield. Whereas infantry training in World War II used bull's-eye targets, now soldiers learn to fire at realistic, man-shaped silhouettes that pop into their field of view. That is the stimulus. The trainees have only a split second to engage the target. The conditioned response is to shoot the target, and then it drops. Stimulus-response, stimulus-response, stimulus-response—soldiers or police officers experience hundreds of repetitions. Later, when soldiers are on the battlefield or a police officer is walking a beat and somebody pops up with a gun, they will shoot reflexively and shoot to kill . . . Now, if you're a little troubled by that, how much more should we be troubled by the fact that every time a child plays an interactive point-and-shoot video game, he is learning the exact same conditioned reflex and motor skills."

It is also Mediascope's view that these games are dangerous. A 1993 study asked 357 seventh- and eighth-graders to identify their preferences among five categories of video games. The researchers found that the most popular game category is fantasy violence, with 32 percent of players preferring such games, followed by sports (29 percent), general entertainment (20 percent), human violence (17 percent), and educational games (2 percent). The study also found that boys who play violent games tend to have a lower self-concept in the areas of academic ability, peer acceptance, and behavior. The results, according to the researchers, raise concern about potential "high risk" game-playing habits. Of particular interest is the possible link between playing violent video games and subsequent aggressive behavior. A number of studies have shown such effects, with younger children again being particularly susceptible to influence.

OF COURSE ENTERTAINMENT AND POPULAR CULTURE *ARE* HISTORICALLY VIOLENT

From the Bible, to Sophocles, to Shakespeare, our cultural world has been fraught with images of violence, death, and destruction. As Robert Hewitt Wolfe, of shows such as *Star Trek: Deep Space Nine*, *Futuresport*, and *Gene Roddenberry's Andromeda* explains, "I'm glad to be living in a society where popular entertainment may be World Wrestling Federation or [violent action director] John Woo's films, rather than gladiatorial games, bear baitings, and public executions. So I'd take exception to the idea that entertainment is more violent than ever. When I think of the times when I was a very angry young man and was sorely tempted to do violence to another person, I'm very glad I didn't own a gun. But I've never attacked anyone with my DVD of *The Killer*."

Still, these are complex, dynamic issues and relationships. They are not amenable to simple absolute conclusions. For instance, it is the already disturbed psyches of youths who have been regularly traumatized who are mostly vulnerable to retraumatization through the media. The most relevant information from the research is that movie and television violence can harm vulnerable segments of society. Many of us might feel gripped by fear for a while after watching traumatizing and violent scenes, feel we are living in a scary world, or become increasingly numb to it, but most of us will not be moved to violence. Unfortunately, this is not the case with some disturbed youth, who can be moved to action.

We do not need overwhelming proof beyond a reasonable doubt about the effects of violence in the media to take action. We don't need to know with 100 percent certainty whether certain images or messages directly cause violence or suffering, or whether others heal. Nevertheless, we need to ask useful questions and search for reliable information. We must challenge ourselves to improve our awareness, our analysis, and our understanding. Most importantly, as a matter of principle, we need to put reliable and meaningful information at the service of morals, ethics, integrity, and common sense. We would do well, at any rate, to use whatever we can learn to reduce suffering and to expand healing.

And just as the entertainment industry has acted in the past to change public consciousness about cancer, child abuse, and domestic violence, it is just beginning to do some of that in the areas of trauma and violence.

9

ENGAGING THE HEALING VORTEX IN ENTERTAINMENT

The story about Mothers Against Drunk Driving (MADD) is a great example of what the entertainment industry can do to radically change social attitudes. MADD was created in 1980. "By the fall of 1982, more than seventy MADD chapters were operating, primarily initiated by victims searching for a way to bring some sense to the apparently meaningless deaths and injuries of their loved ones," according to the MADD website. In March 1983, NBC's *The Candy Lightner Story*, a made-for-television movie about the founder of MADD, resulted in 122 more chapters opening in 35 states. By the end of that month, 84 percent of the country had heard about MADD and 55 percent believed MADD was accomplishing its mission. Today there are 600 chapters and Community Action Teams throughout the 50 states.

Since MADD's inception, alcohol-related traffic deaths have declined 43 percent, allowing for an estimated 138,000 people to be alive today. As a result of its efforts and the unwavering support it has received from the media, an untold number of victims receive assistance in dealing with the aftermath of alcohol-related auto accidents. A positive learning curve is possible when the public is provided with information. Dissemination of information—"the public has the right to know"—is what the media is committed to as its mission. In the case of MADD, what the public had the right to know changed behavior and enhanced well being.

The entertainment industry can create more characters and publicize more stories showing helpful and inspiring behavior and events, including more effective ways to address violence, cruelty, and evil. Witness the public's positive response to the firemen in New York as heroes.

A HEALING ROLE FOR THE MOVIES

Since the dawn of humanity, indigenous cultures have understood the essence of trauma. Its basic nature was captured powerfully in ancient texts, from the Bible to Homer. In the collected myths from around the world, Joseph Campbell relates stories of trauma and healing as natural occurrences in which whole communities participated.

Today, the movie industry is society's storyteller and may well represent our only hope in filling in the gaps of lost community. It may be "a calling" to the media to help restore healing of trauma and to help integrate this natural phenomenon back into the fabric of our lives and our cultures.

Indeed, it seems that a shift has been occurring in the entertainment industry. In movies, the big story of 1999 was the almost complete absence of the big ultra-violent action film. In the mid-1990s, Schwarzenegger, Stallone, and Bruce Willis filled summer screens with an orgy of blood. But as movie themes got more superficial, audiences turned elsewhere. Only the cyberpunk hit *The Matrix* carried a high body count and attracted an audience. *The Blair Witch Project*, the summer's horror hit, though anxiety provoking and emotionally gripping, minimized the display of visual gore and violence. It is a first step. "The public, through ticket sales, showed it is no longer interested in that," says Peter Strauss, president of Lion Gate Films.

The year 2000 featured a surprising number of movies with positive messages about trauma and healing. The wonderful animated children's film *The Iron Giant*, about a robotic super weapon that discovers its soul and decides, "I am not a gun," was filled with deftly delivered anti-violence messages. *The Three Kings* cleverly sold itself as a shoot-'em-up action film, but actually took a strong antiwar stance and de-glamorized violence by showing exactly what bullets do to human bodies. Even the wildly popular supernatural thriller *The Sixth Sense* was at its core the story of a wounded soul's efforts to heal itself by reaching out to another person in need.

PLEASANT SURPRISES ON THE TUBE

At CBS-TV, producer Mark Johnson was learning on the job about this paradigm shift. He had been developing a gritty cop series called *Falcone*. A week after the student massacre at Littleton, he screened the pilot, which included two violent scenes. Says Network president Leslie Moonves, "I don't know if it would have bothered us before, but we had a visceral reaction to someone pulling out a submachine gun." Instead of slotting the series in the fall schedule, Moonves held it as a midseason replacement. Johnson considers the show a victim of bad timing. "I told the director, 'Don't hold back,' when he shot [the two violent] scenes. I thought it would sell better if it pushed the envelope. Today, I certainly wouldn't have done the same thing. Violence doesn't sell."

While many of the more sober news shows (*Dateline NBC, 20/20,* etc.) devote endless hours to gruesome real-life crime stories, such as the Yosemite serial killings and the JonBenet Ramsey case, some of the more heartfelt depictions of trauma and healing take place on TV entertainment shows like *Beverly Hills, 90210* and *Buffy the Vampire Slayer.* The long-term consequences of violence and trauma have been covered by innovative shows like *NYPD Blue, ER,* and *Law and Order.* It is encouraging that many of these programs devote very little actual time depicting the traumatic or violent acts themselves, and instead look at the emotional aftermath and the efforts of professionals to solve the crimes, heal the wounded, and help put lives back together again.

As writer/producer Robert Wolfe explained when he was interviewed for this book, "I've certainly written a lot of straight action/adventure stories, but some of the ones I'm proudest of barely show any violence at all, and instead deal with its consequences on people. I wrote one episode ("Hard Time"), which was about a character who has the memory of a brutal twenty-year prison term planted into his brain, and it's all about him trying to come to terms with his experiences and make sense of them."

When Wolfe was asked whether being the son of a Vietnam combat veteran made him particularly sensitive to stories about trauma and PTSD, he replied: "Of course. It's both something I have very strong feelings about, and also a subject that makes for great stories."

Other excellent television shows get the trauma angle right, each in its own way. They deal with tragedy, violence, and healing in a positive and constructive fashion. Perhaps their writers know what many trauma specialists have realized all along—that loss and healing can be terrifically potent sources of emotionally powerful storytelling. These shows of 1999 include:

- *Boston Public* (Fox). A public school setting allows for many interesting explorations of topics such as school violence, learning disabilities, and how teachers affect their students' lives.

- *7th Heaven* (The WB) This drama, about a mellow minister and his large well-behaved family, has become a surprise hit among young viewers. The show has done an admirable job in tackling hot-button issues such as gun violence and family strife as well.

- *Law and Order; Law and Order: Special Victims Unit* (NBC) Difficult going in places, but these two topical programs about violent crimes and the people who investigate them could never be mistaken for glamorizing violence and trauma.

- *Once and Again* (ABC) Recovery from divorce and its effects on parents and their children is the theme of this excellent drama from the creators of *ThirtySomething* and *My So-Called Life*.

- *Party of Five* (Fox) The very premise deals with recovery from trauma: five siblings, ages two to twenty-five, must raise themselves after their parents are killed in a drunk-driving accident. Other episodes have heaped sorrows aplenty on the young Salinger clan, who always manage to stick together and overcome their problems through cooperation and their mutual understanding.

- *Buffy the Vampire Slayer* (The WB) Before you laugh at Buffy's inclusion, consider this: When was the last time a television show depicted teenagers and young adults as compassionate, brave, and willing to risk their lives for each other and for the greater good of humanity? Kickboxing and supernatural beasties have been sandwiched between some powerful meditations on grief, loss, and atonement for past wrongs.

- *Beverly Hills, 90210* (Fox) Divorce, rape, suicide, childhood sexual abuse; the photogenic young people of this long-running teen soap dealt with them all, and the now departed *90210's* producers did an admirable job of bringing in expert consultants to help them handle each storyline in a socially responsible manner.

- *Freaks and Geeks* (NBC) Surviving high school may not rank with fires, floods, or Bosnian war atrocities, but this wonderfully written show helps all of us who still bear emotional scars from our teenage years to laugh and learn along with its hapless characters.

The good news extends beyond these drama series. In late 1998, MTV, which banned guns in music videos several years ago, debuted a comprehensive anti-violence initiative. "Fight for Your Rights: Take a Stand Against Violence" opened with a special edition of MTV News' *True Life*, a weekly documentary series about the lives and concerns of young adults. In *True Life: Matthew's Murder*, MTV News reporter Serena Altschul investigated Matthew Shepard's murder and examined violence against gays and lesbians across the country. Other such programming continues both on the air and at MTV's popular website.

One night in August 1999, the nation's major television networks, in concert with the White House, blanketed the airwaves with a message urging parents to talk with their children about violence in the wake of shootings at public schools and a community center. In a public service announcement which aired on more than two dozen networks between eight and nine o'clock, former President Clinton said: "Our children need our help to deal with tough issues like violence. Please, talk with your kids." The Ad Council called the coordinated effort "unprecedented," saying it reached millions of viewers during the family hour of TV programming. Such announcements have continued to air. Two years later, on the anniversary date of the September 11 attacks, First Lady Laura Bush exhorted the nation to not stay glued to the television and watch the repetitive running of the Twin Towers' collapse. Major national figures taking on causes with the exposure of media coverage serve the public and have a great impact on people.

Similarly to the major television networks, the makers of violent video games have responded by building in parental controls. Parents can now set the ultra-bloody *Kingpin: Life of Crime* to run at a lower level of brutality and kids need a password to change levels. "That was totally a direct response to Columbine," says Doug Lowenstein, president of the Interactive Digital Software Association.

SPECIFIC WAYS THE ENTERTAINMENT MEDIA CAN ENCOURAGE THE HEALING VORTEX

According to media literacy educator Barbara Osborn, violence is the foundation of many films, TV movies, and action series. "In fact," she explains, "violence is often synonymous with 'action.'" How can the entertainment industry play down violence and encourage the healing vortex? The following suggestions might prove helpful:

- Recognize that ratings alone, important as they are, cannot be the bottom line. Luckily, the public seems ready to cooperate in the changes so that covering the healing vortex can also be lucrative. Many viewers—older people, women, and concerned parents—steer clear of or turn off violent programming.

- Create more characters and stories showing helpful and inspiring behavior and events, including more effective ways to address violence, cruelty, and evil.

- Avoid stories in which violence drives the story line. Barbara Osborn cautions programmers to pay attention to whether there would be a story without the violence. "A crime, a murder, and a fistfight are used to launch TV and movie plots. Violence is often the very pretext for the action that follows."

- Portray violence in a manner that does not encourage it. For instance, programs could show the public the consequences to the perpetrators of violent acts, as well as the physical suffering of the victims. This also means avoiding violent behavior where the consequences to the perpetrators and the victims are not shown. When neither regrets nor grief over violent acts are expressed, this negatively influences impressionable and troubled people. According to Barbara Osborn, "The real world consequences of violence—the physical handicaps, financial expense, and emotional cost—are never a part of the plot. Perhaps the most chilling aspect of the media's portrayal of violence is that when people are killed, they simply disappear. No one mourns his or her death. Their lives are unimportant."

- Avoid violent scenes which include a clear intention to harm or injure; portrayals of physical and verbal abuse; violence that leaves the viewer in an aroused state; violence that is uninterrupted and not subjected to critical commentary; violence portrayed realistically. All of these scenarios influence the viewer who is already predisposed to act aggressively;

- Avoid portrayals of well-intentioned heroes who use violence and aggressive behavior that seem justified. Children are highly influenced by the actions of characters they can identify with and by violence that has cues similar to those in real life.

- Create complex characters rather than cardboard "good guys" and "bad guys." To enlist viewers' emotions, writers must quickly contrast good and evil. "Deeper, more realistic, more ambiguous characterizations make it hard for viewers to know whom to root for," explains Barbara Olson. "It also requires more screen time that takes away from on-screen action. As a result, TV and film criminals are reduced to caricatures.[. . .] No one could care about them. They have no families. Many of them don't even have full names, only nicknames. They deserve no sympathy and they get what they deserve." Why does the good guy beat up on them? Obviously, because they're "bad guys."

- Understand that humor combined with violence trivializes the viewers' perceptions of the violence and its consequences.

- Promote people who show courage, dedication, and heroism as having both entertainment and news value.

- Tell stories with a healing message and showing how people have successfully recovered from tragedies.

- Promote stories that encourage connections between people and their communities.

As the entertainment industry engages tools of the healing vortex with increasing regularity, it can become more sophisticated in designing creative and powerful material that fuels the healing vortex and engages the industry and the public in the ultimate win-win scenario.

10

TRAUMA IS CURABLE

"Trauma may be a fact of life but it doesn't have to be a life sentence." Peter Levine's words echo the belief that we do not have to be condemned to cling to the traumatic past and to relive its devastating events again and again. *Trauma is curable!* This is the first message that the media can deliver to the public at large.

Individuals and nations can heal from trauma and the media can play an important role in giving impetus to the healing vortex. It is crucial that people be helped to understand that they might be caught in the trauma vortex; to provide them with the knowledge on how to best cope with trauma; to help them reignite hope and reestablish dreams; and to help them direct themselves toward life-affirming beliefs.

It is important that we collectively bring awareness around the real nature of traumatic reactions. It is imperative to understand that individuals and countries oscillate between the two vortexes—from hope, optimism, energy, and altruism, to fatigue, frustrations, disillusionment, and polarized thinking—and back again.

Media can participate in facilitating this awareness individually and nationally by:

- Shedding light on the pull of the trauma vortex;
- Explaining the need to encourage the healing vortex through support groups and safe forums to vent anger and frustrations;

147

- Helping people develop or reconnect with their individual or national resources, with all the elements of culture or individual life that offer a calming and healing effect.

THE BASICS OF TRAUMA HEALING

In the last several years, the scientific community has developed a number of techniques that help traumatized individuals release and master traumatic events, memories, and patterns, manage their hyperarousal, and contain their explosiveness and sensitivity. We now have the tools to reawaken the body's innate capacity for resilience and return it to a state of dynamic equilibrium.

The same immense energies that created the symptoms of trauma can also be used to propel us toward healing and mastery. With these proactive interventions, trauma's momentum can be reversed and the equally dynamic upward cycle generated.

In order to remain healthy, all animals (including humans) must discharge the vast energies mobilized to handle survival situations. This discharge completes our activated responses to threat and allows us to return to normal functioning or to reach homeostasis in our nervous system. All organisms have the capacity to respond appropriately to any given circumstance and then return to a base line. For most people, such completion occurs automatically, especially when their environment is supportive.

For those whose process remains unresolved, however, healing requires a pro-active initiative. People who have lived with trauma for a long time usually feel hopeless about ever getting better. They are resigned or desperate because they do not know or believe that there are effective treatments available. They might not even know that their feelings are products of trauma. But we do know that with a commitment to heal and to strengthen the "healing vortex," the body's downward spiral can be reversed. Just understanding that one's symptoms are related to trauma can help put them in perspective and help individuals better cope with them.

Trauma can be released and healed through corrective emotional and sensorial experiences, as well as corrective thinking. The remarkable plasticity of the brain allows us to rewire and repattern our perceptions, memories, and physiological reactions so that we can make psychological and physical peace with the past. Following are some healing principles relevant to the general public.

GENERAL TIPS FOR HEALING TRAUMA

Healing Begins with Accurate Information

Realizing the normal responses to abnormal events may be the first tool for healing that needs to be understood in order to develop health, according to the steps outlined in APA article, *"Managing Traumatic Stress,"* and the theory of Somatic Experiencing.

Understanding the range of responses to trauma can aid in coping effectively with trauma-generated feelings, thoughts, and behaviors. There is no one "standard" reaction to the extreme stress of traumatic experience. Some people respond immediately, while others have delayed reactions. Some have adverse effects for a long period of time, while others recover quickly.

It is common for people who have experienced traumatic situations to have intense emotional reactions. Too often, however, there is a cultural tendency to disparage these normal feelings in us and in others, perhaps in the name of misplaced heroism or propriety. Frequently, when in the grip of them, we worry that we are crazy or different from everybody else; we feel ashamed for being deficient or guilty for losing control.

Shock and denial are also typical responses to disaster and other kinds of trauma, especially shortly after the event. Both are normal protective reactions. We also need to understand that we may feel numb or disconnected from life temporarily. As the initial shock subsides, reactions vary from person to person. And reactions can change over time. Some who have suffered from trauma are initially energized by the event to help them cope with life even better, only to later become discouraged or depressed. For others, the opposite is true. Understanding these differences and not judging oneself according to some arbitrary notion of what the right reaction is helps people overcome the shame and embarrassment that are so often companions of trauma.

Resiliency to trauma can be developed

Specific resiliency skills that can help people rebound from trauma can be developed. However, healing and resiliency call for self-awareness. Developing resilience takes practice and self-application. It requires the development of a certain proficiency in the body/mind language. The effort is worthwhile. Indeed, research has shown that individuals who have the capacity to self-observe, also called the "third eye," and articulate their thoughts, feelings, sensations, and behaviors are capable of faster and greater healing.

Communication and support
are necessary to heal trauma

Trauma tends to make us lose our connection with ourselves, with life, and with others. Yet we must turn to others for support and resist the urge to go it alone. Breaking the isolation is a first and important step, as well as asking for support from people who care about us and who will listen and empathize with our situation.

Telling someone what happened and our feelings about it, whether it is expressing it to a spouse, friend, family member, clergy member, or a therapist, starts the healing process even if it does not resolve all our issues. It is crucial to let other people in.

However, we need to keep in mind that our typical support system may be weakened if those who are close to us have experienced or witnessed the same trauma or are impacted by the effects of our trauma. In addition, we must be aware that in moving toward healing, we may need to return again and again to the recollection of the event or experience it until our environment can integrate the information.

Furthermore, understanding that comparing one's traumatic reactions to those of others is not only futile but also downright harmful. Learning to process trauma from within the framework of one's own experiences will save many people from self-conscious shame; when we don't understand the nature of trauma and confuse it with being crazy, we are tempted to deny that we, or a person close to us, are traumatized.

For example, Esther had been assaulted twice in one year. Her husband Fred, who had been assaulted three times himself, felt the events had no effect on him. He was adamant that there was nothing wrong with his wife Esther and therefore refused to let her take any medication for her panic attacks or go into therapy. Fortunately for both of them, and for Esther's recovery, Fred's sister was a trauma therapist who normalized the situation for them and encouraged Esther to take the initiative and begin therapy and medication. When traumatic symptoms are understood and normalized for the general public through the media, attitudes like Fred's will disappear.

Community involvement is also important in dealing with traumatic disasters. Finding out about local support groups that are available, such as for those who have suffered from natural disasters, victims of rape, or for parents who have lost a child, is important and helpful. These can be especially helpful for people with limited personal support systems. Joining groups led by appropriately trained and experienced professionals and participating in group discussion can help people realize that other individuals in the same circumstances often have similar reactions and emotions and can expose them to more tools and resources. It is also crucial to understand that trauma-based groups are useful only for a certain period of time; otherwise group participants develop a victim-based identity.

Sometimes support can be spontaneous and culturally based. For example, after Southern California's Northridge earthquake, groups in the Latino community fared better than other victims who went to emergency shelters. Specialists in trauma speculated this occurred because many Latinos stayed together, camping outside their homes. They engaged in daily activities and were close to nature.

Break the pull of the trauma vortex

Unresolved trauma tends to narrow our vision of life and our sense of hope and future. We become mired in a sea of negative and hopeless feelings, and we focus only on what is related to the trauma. Awareness can get us out of that state of narrow focus. We must concentrate on what is positive around us, even if trauma tugs at our consciousness like a persistent toothache. Understanding trauma's pull helps us not only become more self-aware but also supports us in taking responsibility for dealing with the experiences and emotions trauma brings.

Deal with emotions without judgment

Emotions such as terror, grief, guilt, helplessness, and anger must be processed and released. This can be done by acknowledging these emotions without judgment and by tracking the sensations they bring up in our bodies. Just observing the sensations helps release them. Positive thoughts and imagery can be called to replace obsessive, negative thoughts. Remembering the resources we have—any memory of a place, person, or event that is calming or brings a feeling of safety—can be helpful. Some people are helped by writing a letter, for their eyes only, to express their experience fully. Journal writing, over time, is another way to gain perspective on oneself and one's experiences.

Feel compassion for self and for others

It is important to forgive others and ourselves. Most of the time, a sign of healed trauma is the ability to feel compassion and forgiveness. Both interrupt the cycle of trauma.

Attitude and spirituality are vital tools

Between denial and defeat there is a point of balance that supports healing. Indeed, there has been much positive research about the power of attitude in healing. The words of theologian Rheinhold Niebuhr, adopted by Alcoholics Anonymous, express this well: "God grant me serenity to accept the things I cannot change; courage to change the things I can; and wisdom to know the difference—living one day at a time; enjoying one moment at a time; accepting hardships as the pathway to peace."

Being in the moment is another path to trauma healing. There are methods that allow us to bring ourselves into the present. For most people, the inspiration gained from spirituality is an essential part of the healing process. Some find this connection through organized religion, some through spiritual groups and practices, and others on their own. Connection with the spirit promotes healing of the mind and body. Furthermore, trauma healing is one of the recognized paths to spiritual transformation.

Self-care has a role in healing trauma

Be kind to yourself. It is important to protect yourself from situations or schedules of extreme stress; to care for your body's needs, to eat right, and sleep well; to be more conscious of self-medicating with tobacco, alcohol, and drugs; to treat yourself to simple gifts—a massage, taking time to read a book in the middle of the day, listening to music, or going for a walk in nature.

> Trauma's pull will be more powerful and its symptoms more intense when you are stressed, fatigued, or ill.

Engage in healthy behaviors to enhance your ability to cope with excessive stress. Eat well-balanced meals and get plenty of rest. If you experience ongoing difficulties with sleep, you may be able to find some relief through relaxation techniques.

Sara is a good example of the results of the healing vortex. She was lucky to have been knowledgeable about trauma's effects when she went through a traumatic divorce—with very little warning, her husband left her for another woman. She noticed that her occasional glass of wine with a meal was turning into a bottle almost every night. Aware that alcohol was a form of self-medication, she stopped drinking and called a therapist.

Establish or reestablish routines such as eating meals at regular times and following an exercise program. Take some time off from the demands of daily life by pursuing hobbies or other enjoyable activities.

Exercise is a good antidote

Stress and anxiety often disappear during physical activity. Most people are aware of the physical benefits of exercise: heart-lung conditioning, weight control, bone and joint strengthening. Regular exercise also improves mood by producing positive biochemical changes in the body and brain. It reduces the amount of adrenal hormones the body releases in response to stress and causes the brain to release greater amounts of powerful, mood-elevating endorphins, producing the sensation familiar to many athletes as "runner's high."

Breathing is the bridge between body and mind

Breathing is the only function that connects the voluntary and involuntary nervous system, forming a bridge between our inner and outer selves. It can be key in trauma prevention. During traumatic stress, dysfunctional respiratory patterns such as irregular breathing, shallow breathing, increased breathing rate, chest breathing, gasps and sighs, and holding one's breath are common. These patterns are reflected in expressions such as "sigh of relief," "catch my breath," and "gasping for air," which reflect the mind/body interrelationship. Changes in breath patterns affect emotions and thoughts and vice versa.

Indeed, during arousal, chest breathing—activated breathing—dominates. Diaphragmatic breathing, on the other hand, reduces arousal of the sympathetic nervous system and helps us relax. This kind of deep breathing is effective in treating many disorders, including trauma, panic attacks, hypertension, and hyperventilation.

Paying attention to one's breathing is probably the simplest, most immediate path to the body's natural "relaxation response," reducing stress and promoting calm. Clients are constantly amazed when they realize that, most of the time, just by paying attention to their shortness of breath and the other sensations in the body that manifest their anxiety, their breathing regulates and gets deeper, and the anxiousness disappears. Beyond simple breathing awareness, there are a number of relaxation techniques, including meditation, that focus on breath control. Specialists go as far as saying that if people do not lose control of their breathing during a traumatic event, they will not be traumatized.

Connecting with nature's deep rhythms is the most available remedy

For most people, time spent in nature—a walk in a park or on the beach, taking in a beautiful sunset, or gazing into the nighttime sky—is healing. The simple act of breaking usual unconscious patterns of behavior, sounds, sights, and rhythms tends to bring us more into the present. Nature can help us experience a sense of connection with our surroundings, a greater awareness of our bodies, and some relief from mental chatter or emotional unease. Even just reminiscing about a pleasant experience in the past can make a positive difference. Connecting with the deeper rhythms of nature allows us to reconnect with our own instinctual rhythms. People need to know that when they are stuck in the trauma vortex, they naturally shy away from nature; they must make a special effort to go into nature to break the hold of the vortex.

Understanding the time factor required for recovery

Time required for recovery will depend on the degree of intensity, the loss suffered, and the level of resiliency of the person. Clearly, events that last longer and pose a greater threat, and where loss of life or substantial loss of property is involved, often take longer to resolve. Trauma caused by people's maliciousness or evil leaves a stronger impact and requires more commitment and time to heal. A person's general ability to cope with emotionally challenging situations will affect the speed of recovery. Individuals who have handled previous difficult, stressful circumstances may well find it easier to cope with the trauma.

Circumstances before and after trauma can affect recovery

Other stressful events preceding the traumatic experience also can influence the outcome. Individuals faced with other emotionally challenging situations, such as serious health problems or family-related difficulties, may have more intense reactions to the new stressful event and may need more time to recover.

Patience with oneself during this process is a great and necessary kindness. Empathy for the traumatized is also crucial, whether for yourself or someone else. Adopting the attitude of allowing for whatever time it takes to heal from trauma takes a tremendous pressure off the traumatized person and speeds recovery. Any judgment associated with the healing process will impede it or slow it down.

Kora had been in a serious accident a year previous, and she had suffered from slight brain damage. Nine months later her mother died unexpectedly from accelerated cancer and her brother got divorced. She felt she was handling everything well and keeping her emotions under control. She had a wonderful support system and felt the deep love of all those who surrounded her. She did not expect to feel overwhelmed when, five months later, her husband had to be hospitalized overnight for kidney stones. She got depressed and could not stop crying. She tried in vain to fight the obsessive thought that bad things would never stop happening to her and was very upset with herself for "being weak and unreasonable."

Kora, her family, and her friends were stunned that such a minor problem as her husband's kidney stones would leave her so prostrated, when in fact she had shown strength and resolution after all the serious traumas she had gone through. Luckily, a more trauma-aware friend of hers normalized Kora's feelings for her. She explained to her how she had gone through accumulated layers of traumatic stress, and throughout it all she had coped well, as her husband had been the rock of Gibraltar—supporting her steadily the whole time. The fact that something could happen to him, her main support system, destabilized her completely and brought the previous stress to the fore.

Being able to face horror

Individuals and society must learn to cope with some of the unbelievable horrors mankind is capable of; we must not distance ourselves from the traumatized, thereby bringing denial in. As a society, we must develop the resiliency to hear and see horror without denying it, without becoming callous to it, nor blaming the victim for it.

Allowing ourselves to feel grief

We must allow ourselves to mourn the losses we've experienced as a result of trauma. There must be room for normal grief, for tears, and for regrets over loss. During the healing process, we often experience grief over the loss of time when life felt so dreary and its potential unlived. If we allow ourselves to feel the grief without judgment, we soon get over it and make the best of what's left. It is helpful to be patient with changes in our emotional state and not berate ourselves for them.

Avoiding major life decisions

Switching careers or jobs, divorcing, or moving tend to be highly stressful activities. When coming on the heels of a personal disaster, we must be aware that these decisions can be trauma driven.

Alexandra and Jeffrey had had a rocky relationship for the past two years of their marriage. The September 11 tragedy was the last straw on their already stressed family system. Alexandra decided to leave the marriage immediately, despite the fact that their financial situation made it very difficult for her. When she became aware of the impact of trauma, she relented and initiated marital therapy with her husband.

USING INTERNAL AND EXTERNAL RESOURCES IS VITAL IN HEALING TRAUMA

Resources help us feel more in charge of ourselves and help us recuperate the control we lost. They help us overcome trauma much faster by helping us feel calmer and stronger and by stabilizing our nervous system. Resources are always present, but trauma makes us forget them. It is vital to refocus on what's healthy for us and within us.

External resources can range from the hug of a loved one or a conversation with a good friend, to being in nature, taking a walk, or watching the movement of the wind in the trees; it can be engaging in favorite activities. External resources also are all organizations that can come to our help. Internal resources include our innate capacities, such as sense of humor, ability to be flexible, creativity, persistence, problem-solving capacity, compassion, and forgiveness. Anything that gives hope and reinforces our healing vortex and our innate capacity to heal is a resource.

Time and our bodies are resources. Allowing time for our nervous system to recuperate is one of the most helpful steps we can take. Body awareness, as we'll see below, allows us to handle nervous system activation in a more helpful manner.

Resources that enable us to master traumatic situations might not be available at the time of the event. But in healing trauma, we can import resources from the present into past situations, from the past into present situations; we can import resources from one situation into another; we can use imaginary resources as well.

For example, at the age of eighteen, Jody lost her mother to cancer. The loss was very traumatizing for her, as she had always felt isolated and alienated from her family, except for her relationship with her mom. Her mother's funeral was particularly harrowing, with people aggregated in several different groups. Jody was by herself. Every time she thought of her mother or the funeral, she would feel overcome with deep sadness, loneliness, tears, and self-pity. She continued to relive the event, every time she heard about or attended a funeral, and felt abandoned and alone all over again, though she was married to a man she loved dearly and had two children.

Fifteen years later, in therapy, she introduced her present resources into the past situation. She brought to her mind's eye her husband and children and a solid, albeit small, group of friends that stood by her in the funeral parlor. She felt the resource of her support system, grounding the sensations of support in her body. After that session, she never felt overcome by depressive feelings again when she thought of her mother and her funeral.

It is important to understand the need to switch back and forth between the story of the trauma and moments of resource. When trauma victims talk about any thing, animal, person, or place that encourages their feelings of calmness, safety, and strength, it will help them remain more stable and allow them to process what happened to them without retraumatizing themselves.

It is also helpful to establish a resource inventory. The more resources we build, the more resilient we become and the faster we recover from our trauma. Missing resources are what we need to add to our list to feel stronger and safer: whether it is a self-defense class for a rape victim, joining a church or group for someone who feels isolated, reconnecting with families, getting a job, and so on.

It is useful to be aware that trauma makes us more resistant to using our resources and we need to make a conscious effort to do it, as there is a natural fixation on trauma.

Creating corrective experiences

We can teach our brains to feel safe, powerful, and in control by imagining an experience of empowerment and resolution and grounding it in the nervous system, to counteract the experience of utter helplessness we felt during a traumatic event. We can increase the resilience of our nervous systems by developing resources grounded in the body as sensations. We need to recognize and understand the power of the process of using all resources, including corrective ones, and the need for allowing ourselves the necessary time to do it.

Recognizing signs of the healing vortex

Signs of the healing vortex that allow a person optimal functioning include:

- Better orienting, feeling lighter, open, spacious, expanded;

- Fuller abdominal breathing, flowing, rhythm, fluidity, gentle waves of energy;

- Better coordination and integration;

- Connectedness to self, others, and nature;

- Feeling more settled, slowed down, calm, and relaxed;

- Feeling centered, more balanced, better grounded, feeling one's weight, heavy in a good way;

- Completion or discharge of incomplete flight responses, such as pushing away or breaking a fall with one's hand slowly and with a sense of safety, settling insights, acceptance, and compassion;

- Sense of power and safety, more options, and more choices;
- Sense of completion, that things are okay internally, depth and clarity.

THE SYMPTOMS OF TRAUMA IN CHILDREN

The intense anxiety and fear that often follow a disaster or other traumatic event can be especially troubling for children. We need to watch for any unusual behavior after a traumatic event. The signs of trauma for children can be the following:

Behavioral: Some may regress and demonstrate earlier behaviors such as thumb sucking, wanting the breast again, bedwetting, or losing toilet-training ability (it is very important to not pressure them to be toilet-trained). Other symptoms include withdrawal, excessive shyness, clinginess, emotional outbursts, aggressiveness with other kids, nightmares, avoidant behavior, and phobias. Compulsive repetitive behavior may include repetitive patterns in play, persistent controlling behavior, hyperactivity, a tendency to startle easily, thrashing in bed, and forgetfulness. Traumatized children may be more prone to nightmares and may fear sleeping alone. They may throw tantrums more frequently or become more solitary. Performance in school may suffer; school phobia is a common way of showing the need for reassurance regarding safety.

Physical: They may manifest physical symptoms, such as headaches, tummy aches, diarrhea, etc. If these symptoms persist, parents or therapists should look for the emotional components.

HELPING TRAUMATIZED CHILDREN

It is possible to help children renegotiate their trauma through play. They can set up the potential for their healing through their own play and master an experience that left them overwhelmed. Parents can help by directing the child's awareness to his/her sensations. In using the principles of charging and discharging, the arousal cycle, and the importance of timing (see below), parents can help their children move out of trauma. If the symptoms come in clusters and last a long time, it's vital to get outside help. Children outgrow these problems, but the energy can still be there. If we remind the child in later years of an unresolved but forgotten trauma, it can be reawakened.

There are several things parents and others who care for children can do to help alleviate the emotional consequences of trauma:

- Spend more time with them and let them be more dependent during the months following the trauma. Physical affection is comforting to traumatized children, so allow your child to cling to you more than usual.

- Provide play experiences to help relieve tension. Younger children in particular may find it easier to share their ideas and feelings about the event through non-verbal activities, such as drawing and play-acting.

- Encourage older children to talk about their thoughts and feelings. This helps reduce confusion and anxiety related to the trauma. Respond to questions in terms they can comprehend. Reassure them repeatedly that you care about them and that you understand their fears and concerns.

- Keep regular schedules for activities such as eating, playing, and bedtimes to help restore a sense of security and normalcy.

For children with prolonged reactions that disrupt daily functioning—such as continual and aggressive emotional outbursts, serious problems at school, preoccupation with the traumatic event, continued or extreme withdrawal, and other signs of intense anxiety or emotional difficulties—there is a need for professional assistance. A qualified mental health professional can help such children and their parents understand and deal with thoughts, feelings, and behaviors that result from trauma. (See Bibliography and Resources for helpful suggestions.)

11

BREAKTHROUGHS
IN TREATMENT

Researchers are struggling more actively than ever to unravel traumatic stress in the aftermath of terrorism. This chapter is an introduction to cutting-edge trauma healing techniques. These techniques have for the most part proven quick, easy, and effective, with wide applicability both in the range of the trauma they heal and the institutions they can assist.

COGNITIVE BEHAVIORAL TREATMENTS AND EXPOSURE THERAPY

Cognitive Behavioral Therapy is a focused, problem-solving approach developed by Aaron T. Beck in the 1970s. It is direct and potent, and its efficacy has been empirically validated for the treatment of PTSD. It identifies thoughts (automatic or unconscious), assumptions, and core beliefs that produce negative or painful feelings as well as maladaptive behaviors. It relies on changing the thinking, which then changes the emotions and behavior. Behavioral techniques are also used, such as relaxation techniques, anger management, assertiveness training, and gradual exposure to the feared situations. The treatment is usually brief. Many qualified therapists practice CBT in the U.S. and around the world.

Jeffrey E. Young, a protégé of Dr. Beck, developed Schema-Focused Cognitive Therapy, an offshoot of CBT. This technique is useful with people who have longstanding self-defeating patterns, themes, or schemas in thinking and feeling. It combines CBT, experiential, interpersonal, and psychoanalytic therapies into a unified model of treatment.

Exposure Therapy is the invention of Dr. Edna B. Foa, professor of clinical psychology and psychiatry at the University of Pennsylvania. She is one of the leading experts in the area of PTSD, and her program for rape victims is considered to be one of the most effective therapies for trauma. Foa believes that if the person is encouraged to expose herself, despite the difficulty to do so, to the traumatic images while in the presence of the therapists for as long as is needed, the fear of these images will disappear.

MEDICATION

Medication is available for reducing overwhelming symptoms of arousal (sleep disturbances and exaggerated startle reflex, intrusive thoughts, avoidance, depression, and panic) and for improving impulse control and behavioral problems. Presently, drug companies are attempting to develop medication that may be stress-protective. It is strongly suggested that medication be accompanied by therapy. Please note that many medications for trauma have mild to significant side effects.

INNOVATIVE TECHNIQUES

Although the family of Cognitive Behavioral Therapies have been the most successfully acknowledged techniques for healing trauma in the past, a new wave of body-centered therapies have appeared in the last fifteen years or so and have permeated the clinical field. These cutting-edge techniques have introduced and begun to integrate the missing component of the body from the previous therapies into the field of trauma.

This is important because we now know that trauma is in the body and not only in the mind. Neuroscience discoveries are providing a scientific foundation for somatic psychotherapy and body-based treatment of trauma and dissociation. The understanding of how neural networks function allows us to understand the relationship between mind and body, why traumatic stress can be healed through the body, and how psychological change can occur.

Over the last two decades, several innovative treatment methods that are proving particularly effective against the ravages of trauma have emerged. Most of these techniques are applicable to a broad range of symptoms including grief and loss, panic, anxiety, phobias, depression, pain, and addiction. These tools can offer dramatic results, sometimes within a few sessions. They draw upon our own resources and inherent capacity to heal. Both external and internal resources are extremely important in this work and time is devoted to helping people identify them.

Some of these tools work well in the hands of dedicated lay people, especially those in the addiction field. Some can be self-applied and some can even be taught via the media in emergency collective situations. There is an ever-growing field of these therapies, but most remain to be supported by research. Only a handful are covered in this chapter. I start with the technique that I believe seems to have most mass application: Somatic Experiencing can be added to most methods and is one of the few techniques that is culturally transportable. It has both an elaborate and detailed theory of trauma, as well as a method for coping with and healing trauma.

Somatic Experiencing (SE)

Trauma is the interaction between the traumatic event and the response of our nervous system to it, creating a disturbance in the larger flow of life experience. To describe our emotional life, Dr. Peter A. Levine, creator of SE, offers the image of a river, in which trauma, like an eddy split off from the mainstream of the river by a storm, represents a region of experiential and energetic flow that has been separated from the rest of experience. To heal the effects of trauma, the individual must integrate the split-off parts back into the larger flow of life experience and eliminate the repetitive and reinforcing associations and triggers.

According to Levine, trauma is an interrupted process that is otherwise naturally inclined to complete itself whenever possible. It is based upon the realization that wild animals, though threatened routinely by predators, are rarely traumatized. They utilize innate mechanisms to regulate and discharge the high levels of energy aroused during defensive survival behaviors.

In *Waking the Tiger: Healing Trauma,* Levine cites the story of a frightened bear in the *National Geographic* video "Polar Bear Alert." Chased down by a pursuing airplane, the bear is shot with a tranquilizer dart, surrounded by wildlife biologists, and then tagged. As the massive animal comes out of its state of shock, it begins to tremble lightly; the trembling intensifies steadily, then peaks into a nearly convulsive shaking, its limbs flailing seemingly at random. The shaking subsides, and the animal takes three deep spontaneous breaths that spread throughout its body.

When viewed in slow motion, it becomes apparent that the "random" leg gyrations are actually coordinated running movements. It is as though the animal completes its escape, actively simulating running movements that were interrupted at the moment it was tranquilized. The animal discharges the "frozen energy," then surrenders in a spontaneous full-bodied breath.

"When animals in the wild come out of this freeze response, they physically discharge the frozen arousal through subtle or gross motor activity, like the bear, and then quickly regain full control of their bodies, returning to normal life as if nothing happened. This understanding of why animals in the wild are not traumatized even though their lives are threatened routinely has provided us a key to healing trauma. When the options of fight or flight are impossible responses to a threatening situation, our ancient biological response is to freeze. "Our healing lies in our natural ability to internally thaw those frozen moments," says Dr. Levine.

Humans possess regulatory mechanisms virtually identical to those in animals. But these mechanisms are often overridden by the rational mind, the neo-cortex. This higher brain function can inhibit the complete discharge of survival energies, which then block the nervous system from regaining equilibrium. Such blockages keep the body stuck in survival mode and retard its attempt to manage or contain this unused energy.

SE works with the implicit and explicit levels of trauma. Explicit means the trauma is held in the consciousness; implicit means the trauma is held at the body level, most likely outside of one's awareness. However, its main techniques work on the implicit level so this treatment is able to reach the deeper levels of trauma by engaging all of the brain levels, from the reptilian to the neo-cortex. Overwhelming feelings of helplessness, fear, rage, confusion, guilt, shame, self-blame, and disorientation all mitigate against self-regulation. When we experience terrible feelings, we tend to recoil and avoid them. We split off or disassociate from them. We fear being consumed by them and brace and tighten our bodies against them. The more we resist, the more these feelings persist. What is not felt does not get processed and remains unchanged or intensified, hence the vicious cycle of trauma.

SE teaches a subtle distinction between sensations, feelings, thoughts, and emotions. We learn how to use the "felt sense"—awareness of internal experience in response to external experience—to navigate the inner landscape of the body. Individuals are guided into the body's instinctive survival energies, previously locked in the neuromuscular and central nervous systems, so these can then be discharged and completed.

The "felt sense," coined originally by Dr. Eugene T. Gendlin, is the tool that allows humans to do what animals do: complete our innate biological processes. It allows us to be in touch with all that is going on with us, at a particular moment, in our body and mind. It is our link between our "highest" and "lowest" functions, between our most elaborate, socialized self and our instinctual self. Learning to sense the entirety of our experience at once, through the felt sense, is an essential element for resolving trauma, as well as for avoiding traumatization. The felt sense gives us the ability to have our sensation-based feelings without being flooded by emotion. This, in turn, enables us to be conscious of the incomplete portion of our defensive and orienting responses. It then allows us to follow the dictates of the reptilian brain and complete whatever response was still stuck in immobility.

The discharge of energies may include:
- Involuntary gentle trembling and shaking vibrations
- Stomach gurgles
- Heat waves
- Warm sweat
- Breathing deeply
- Spontaneous laughter or crying
- Goose pimples

Paradoxically, focusing on uncomfortable sensations for a relatively short period of time relaxes one and allows the body to shift, change, and reestablish its balance. It is this balance that allows the person to evolve toward greater self-esteem. Clients with a history of seven or ten car accidents (trauma reenactment at its best, as the natural instinctive reflexes have been compromised) come in seeking effective treatment. They have gone to all the usual care providers: doctors, chiropractors, masseurs, etc., and still have symptoms, often two or more years later. With Somatic Experiencing, they can usually recover with ten to fifteen sessions.

In *Grace Unfolding*, Ron Kurtz and Greg Johanson prescribe a method for achieving "mindfulness" that embraces the same scientific principles in SE (especially Gendlin's concept of the "felt sense") in a meditation- and Taoist-inspired approach. They write: "A good therapist invites us, as well as herself, to practice mindful non-doing. If we report 'I'm anxious,' questions like 'Why do you think you're anxious?' produce only analysis with effort. There are many ways to encourage a receptive, mindful, non-doing consciousness. These ways are all variations on questions and instructions that direct us back to our experience as the only possible source of knowledge: 'What is the quality of anxiety?' 'Where do you experience the anxiety in your body?' 'What movement does the anxiety promote in you?' 'What does this anxiety tell you about what you need in order to feel less anxious?'

"If, as clients, we can practice staying with our experience, without labeling, judging or criticizing it, observing it without losing touch with it, and reporting on it without coming out of it, the experience has an opportunity to deepen and release."

A balanced nervous system is one in which the parasympathetic autonomic nervous system has recuperated its healthy functioning. Relaxation signals are:

- Slower, deeper respiration
- Slower heart rate and pulse
- Decreased blood pressure

- Constriction of pupils
- Blushed/flushed skin color
- Skin warm and dry to the touch
- Increase in digestion and peristalsis

Rhythm and timing are very important in SE. Everything in nature is dictated by cycles. Animals follow the rhythms of nature. So too do the responses that bring traumatic reactions to their natural resolution. For human beings, these rhythms pose a two-fold challenge. First, they move at a much slower pace than our fast-paced lifestyles; we need to learn to take this time. Second, healing cycles can only be nurtured and validated; they cannot be manipulated, hurried, or forced into change.

Resolving a traumatic reaction not only eliminates the likelihood of symptoms emerging later, but also fosters an ability to move through future threatening situations with greater ease. It helps to generate a natural resiliency to stress.

Three Clients' Testimonials Illustrate the Power of the New Techniques:

When I asked three of my trauma clients the following question: In what way was this therapy different for you from other therapies? I let them answer, without interrupting:

Laura Lee

Laura Lee wanted me to use her real name. "My past therapies were different in that they didn't deal with the body. This one does. I had never heard of the ways animals in the wild release trauma or the functions of the reptilian brain before," she said, "but it made perfect sense to me when it was explained. It just sounded right. Feelings do get stuck, and the energy is trapped. People know that at some level, but we don't know how to use that knowledge. And it's simple; it's easy. It's like learning to paint by numbers—you look at the book *(Waking the Tiger)*, at the pictures he asks you to look at, see how you feel, and realize that each little piece adds up to one big thing at the end.

I was also astounded when you made me stop being angry. I never believed I could stop feeling angry just like that, right in the middle of feeling angry. But I did. I learned that anger is just an emotion. That you have to tell emotions what to do, like children, so they don't run the show, that the amygdala doesn't differentiate between real and unreal emotions.

I feel really happy with this work. I use my mind now in a way I never have before. I communicate with my subconscious mind, and let my body tell me what to do. My mind and body are connected and communicating; before they were separated. I just had all this pain, and now I know what to do to get rid of it. You have to be willing to be crazy, really feel like a freak. No medical doctor in a big building ever told me about all of this before.

If I have pain in my feet now, I have an image of that energy and it will tingle. And the pain is gone. Sometimes I forget to do this and the pain returns for a week. But then I remember again, and it goes away. It is so funny how easily we are disconnected.

Even my diet has changed—I only want to eat fresh, whole foods, nothing canned, packaged, or processed."

Carla

"These techniques are completely different from other forms of therapy. The others were fine, and it helps to talk about things, but this is profound. It reinforces what I already knew, that my body is a well of knowledge. I am connected with my emotional body as well, and I've learned to connect spirit/mind/body in a completely different way. It has made me feel that I have so much power, and that I don't have to be a victim of the traumas of the past.

It is so amazing to learn how to sit with a feeling and watch what's unfolding from it as an insight or thought. There is a dialogue going on between my mind and my body. Sometimes I ask myself: How did this happen? It's amazing how much you discover about yourself just sitting with sensations in your body; how quickly the sensations pass when you give attention to them and how fast you can get rid of a traumatic constriction. The work of retraining the nervous system is really amazing. It gave me the skills to work with myself, to really work through things on my own. I have a completely different relationship with myself as well as with others, that is much more intimate and deep.

I am aware of my behavior patterns much more quickly and I don't judge them. I am much more aware of them now and that they don't serve me. I am so amazed I can move through and shift things so quickly and profoundly. I don't think that can come only with words. This therapy gave me lots of hope and possibilities, and opened up things for me."

Shari

"It is painful for a second, but it just starts to release and come out—my neck feels really loose. I thought I had to go digging but it was just there, at the surface. It feels like spasms or little jerks, movements in my body.

It feels weird, the little movements, but a good weird. It feels good to give up my mind to my body. It feels empty, but not sad; clear, like there is space, expansion. This is amazing! You must enjoy doing this. It's so funny—you don't have to talk about that stuff. Half of the depression was that I was so sick and tired of hearing myself go on [without any resolution]."

Eye Movement Desensitization and Reprocessing (EMDR)

Eye Movement Desensitization and Reprocessing (EMDR), developed by psychologist Francine Shapiro, Ph.D., involves visual, auditory, and kinesthetic bilateral stimulation while the trauma-tized individual processes and reintegrates traumatic material. The person thinks about the traumatic memory and the negative beliefs associated with it ("It was my fault that I got raped") while visu-ally tracking the rapid back-and-forth movements the therapist makes with two fingers or a wand in the line of vision. Alternately, physical taps or sound may be used. Like the eye movements, taps or sounds are alternated left and right. The bilateral stimulation seems to be an essential element of the treatment. It has been speculated that it creates a synapse connecting the stuck material with the innate capacity of the individual to heal.

Shapiro has spent years working to establish EMDR within stan-dard professional and scientific psychology, pushing more stren-uously for empirical research than any other mental health care innovator in recent history (outside the pharmaceutical indus-try). She has provided free EMDR training to researchers and trained more than 50,000 clinicians in her approach all over the world. EMDR has been the subject of at least sixty clinical research studies.

Recent work on the developmental process of creating neural networks that mediate various functions and traumatic memory may provide a plausible mechanism to explain the efficacy of EMDR and other therapeutic approaches which use repetitive, rhythmic sensory stimulation with cognitive recall to treat trauma.

In 1997, Kaiser Permanente, a large California HMO, funded a study comparing EMDR with standard Kaiser psychological care (talk therapy with or without medication) for trauma victims. By the end of the study, nearly 80 percent of the EMDR group no longer suffered from PTSD symptoms, compared with just half of those who got standard care. Not only were more EMDR patients cured, but they recovered twice as quickly. On average, they were symptom-free after just six sessions, as compared to twelve for standard care. Psychological tests also showed that eye-movement therapy did a better job of easing depression and anxiety, with most EMDR patients testing in the normal range after therapy. EMDR is also an excellent tool for processing negative self-beliefs.

Neuro-imaging researcher Bessel Van der Kolk recently investigated the efficacy of EMDR treatment effects. He found that the flashbacks with which several Vietnam veterans had been plagued for over twenty years remitted in a few sessions. After three sessions exactly, their symptoms were greatly relieved. Using MRIs, he found that before treatment, during a provoked flashback, the amygdala of each subject was over-activated and the hippocampus was shut down. After the EMDR treatment that process reversed itself.

Francine's testimony

"You have been telling this for so long, but now I know it from inside. It stays with me. I sat yesterday in a café on Larchmont and for the first time I thought men were okay, that I liked men, that they weren't all bad. The tension and hatred I felt when I thought about my rapes just went away. I can't retrieve the feeling! It is just amazing!"

Traumatic Incident Reduction (TIR)

TIR is a highly focused and repetitive desensitization and cognitive imagery approach that was refined in the mid-1980s by California psychiatrist Frank Gerbode. It is a directive and control-based tool, addressing thoughts, feelings, emotions, and sensations. The process works well with adults and children. In a single session, the client is directed to review a traumatic incident, first silently, then aloud, over and over again, until arriving at an internal resolution. The client is enabled to reach his own insights and resolve his difficulties. The therapist's role is to keep the client's attention tightly focused on the incident. TIR can be applied informally, even though it is structured. Therapists from many different theoretical backgrounds can use it cross-culturally. The technique can also be taught to lay people. The limitations are that one needs to take as long a time as it takes to process a traumatic event in one sitting. Going through the retelling of a traumatic experience repeatedly can be very painful.

Visual Kinesthetic Dissociation (VKD)

VKD, demonstrated by Florida therapists Maryanne and Edward Reese, is related to Neuro-Linguistic Programming (NLP), developed in the early 1970s by Richard Bandler and John Grinder. It is an approach based on close observation of verbal, behavioral, and sensory patterns. In VDK's application of NLP to trauma incidents, clients are led through a step-by-step program of purposeful dissociation from the trauma, watching a "movie" of themselves reliving the traumatic event and instructed to imagine communicating with and reassuring their younger, traumatized selves. The entire experience is thereby integrated into their present lives.

Thought Field Therapy (TFT)

TFT, created by Roger Callahan during the early 1980s, requires only that the client think briefly about the traumatic event while specific acupuncture meridian points (believed to stimulate the body's bio-energy system) are tapped or rubbed. The technique allows traumatic events to loosen their hold on victims. It works to rid clients of their flashbacks, upset emotions, and obsessive thoughts.

Emotional Freedom Technique (EFT)

Emotional Freedom Technique (EFT) is an offshoot of TFT. Gary Craig, a student of Callahan, simplified TFT by creating an all-inclusive sequence that tapped all seven body meridian points. This allowed people to bypass the need for detailed diagnosis. EFT, like TFT, is based on the idea that emotional problems are directly linked to disturbances or blockages in the acupuncture meridian system. Clients who have had successful experiences with it feel transformed and relieved of their pain.

Craig maintains an active list on the Internet of methods based on his approach. He is determined to make EFT available to as many people as possible. Videos and tapes are sold at cost. Treatment is aimed at neutralizing, balancing, or in other ways clearing blockages, often by tapping on or holding acupuncture points while keeping the problem in mind. In my private practice, I have found that children, in particular, have taken very well to the tapping and do it at home, by themselves. Some taught their friends to use it.

Research on the outcomes of power therapies

In a July/August 1996 article, published in the *Networker*, Mary Skyles Wylie examines the efficiency of the above-listed Power Therapies. Her findings showed that the techniques were equivalent in their ability to treat PTSD successfully. According to Gail Davies, director of the psychosocial stress clinic at Florida State, who administered the overall project, "Not one client who participated in the project failed to benefit." In addition to real-world changes, the subjects all showed improvement on tests measuring symptoms and self-assessment. Davies calls it an educational model for helping people achieve personal growth.

External Validation

Many energy psychotherapy conferences have already taken place and the umbrella organization, ACEP (Association for Comprehensive Energy Psychotherapies), is rapidly expanding.

Charles Figley, the founder of the International Society of Traumatic Stress Studies and *The Journal of Traumatic Stress,* coined the concept "secondhand trauma," and has been a leader in the study and treatment of trauma. With his Florida State University colleague, Joyce Carbonell, he oversaw what they termed the "active ingredients" project, which set out to demonstrate and test a number of the new trauma therapies. The project was not intended to compare the approaches to find which one worked best. Rather, it was a pioneering attempt to demonstrate four new methods of treatment on a typical client population in a sufficiently rigorous and controlled way, from which empirically valid conclusions could be drawn. Inventors of each of the methods came together for a week and worked publicly with assigned clients in a laboratory setting. Discussions devoted to assessing the results followed.

Figley and Carbonell created the criteria to evaluate the trauma methods. Approaches had to be "extremely efficient," producing within a few sessions an "extraordinary impact on clients' progress in recovering from PTSD." Effectiveness had to be verified by 200 to 300 licensed or certified clinicians. Suffering the aftereffects of a trauma or a phobia (on the theory that many phobias are embedded reactions to trauma), the majority of the participants were women, median age forty. Nearly 40 percent were dealing with unresolved issues from childhood abuse. The remaining subjects included Vietnam and Gulf War veterans, victims of crime, rape, domestic violence, and accidents, and people suffering bereavement, losses, and phobias.

Of thirty-nine people who made it through the entire process of treatment, the number of participants assigned to each approach ranged from six to fifteen (EMDR: 6; TIR and VKD: 9; TFT: 15). The average time required to achieve results by each method ranged from a high of just over four hours for EMDR (which requires the clients to talk more) to a low of just about one hour for TFT. Clearly, these techniques offer quick relief for traumatic symptoms previously considered most daunting.

The Counting Method

The Counting Method is a technique for modulating and mastering traumatic memories in which the therapist counts out loud to one hundred while the client silently remembers a traumatic event. Immediately afterward the recollection is reported, discussed, and reframed.

The Counting Method has been disseminated through instructional videotape (Ochberg, 1993). It is used in the context of Posttraumatic Therapy, an eclectic approach that includes education, holistic health, social support, and search for meaning. The goal is a realistic, enhanced sense of self, rather than merely symptom reduction. Survivor rather than victim status ("I look back with sadness rather than hate, I look forward with hope rather than despair, I may never forget but I need not constantly remember. I was a victim. I am a survivor;" Ochberg, 1988 is another way of summarizing the goal of Posttraumatic Therapy.

No clients have reported negative consequences attributable to the Counting Method. Approximately 80 percent reported improvement in the frequency and intensity of traumatic memory.

The Counting Method shares some elements of Shapiro's (1989) Eye Movement Desensitization. But scientific determination of the way the method works and how efficacious it is must await controlled outcome study. This research is underway (Johnson, Lubin, Morgan, Grillon, 1995), evaluating clients randomly assigned to therapists cross-trained in Foa's (1991) flooding technique, EMDR, and the Counting Method.

THE WAVE OF THE FUTURE

The current economics of managed care demand shorter therapies, making brief, affordable, and effective treatments attractive. No two people experience PTSD the same way, and there isn't one quick fix that works for every client. The variety of new tools available allow for more flexibility and more customized therapy. These new approaches are techniques and tools that stand on their own or can be integrated in traditional therapies. They all rely on the innate ability of the client to heal.

Therapists know that successful treatment still requires a good therapeutic relationship, and emphasizing the quick symptomatic fix should not bypass that need nor put the field in danger of minimizing treatment. This is why substituting brief trauma therapy for psychotherapy may *not be* sufficient, especially when a person is suffering from developmental trauma. These new therapies are seen as offering hope by jump-starting the process and adding effectiveness. In the context of trauma-based disorders, psychological suffering and neuro-physiological stress must be seen in a larger picture, including situational, social, political, and spiritual issues.

12

FAST-FORWARD
TO A BETTER WORLD

In the mind's eye, let us imagine that it is the year 2030 or 2040. What would change if the public really understood all the information about trauma with the help of the media? This is my vision, my deepest hope:

- The stigma of trauma will be long gone. A man's sense of manhood will no longer be at stake if he acknowledges a traumatic response. People will talk about trauma as they do now about flu and heart disease.

- Traumatic events will still occur, but there will be less criminal violence and no school violence because there will be school courses on developing resiliency to trauma and emotional intelligence training. All school counselors and psychologists will be trained in detecting the psychological effects of trauma and know how to treat it or refer for appropriate treatment.

- Children will be tested for psychological trauma at an early age and won't be misdiagnosed as having learning disabilities, inappropriate aggression, or other pathologies so commonly assigned today. Crack babies, for example, will be given an extraordinary and simple treatment that reestablishes the balance of their nervous system through rhythmic movements.

- Gangs will have disappeared as our modern initiation for disadvantaged youths. Our understanding of the importance of attachment and proper bonding at an early age will have allowed us to create and provide the appropriate courses in maternity wings to new mothers and fathers. Programs will be developed in all communities introducing our youth to initiation rites that are socially approved.

- The number of teenage mothers will diminish significantly, and they will not be treated as social outcasts caught in the welfare system, but helped to recover from their traumas and regain a healthy sense of self that will allow them to take charge of their lives and bring up healthy babies.

- Prostitution will be regarded as possibly a product of trauma in our society and constructive help will be offered instead of scorn and jail.

- Research has shown that more than 40 percent of women on welfare have been sexually abused as young girls. This data will serve to inform the welfare system of the twenty-first century. Welfare recipients will receive governmental help and undergo therapeutic treatment at the same time, including trauma work. Sensitive and well-trained trauma therapists, aware that a high number of these welfare recipients have been either sexually or physically abused, will be able to help them heal from the old wounds that keep them from leading full and independent lives.

- Judges, lawyers, and social workers in the family court system will be well informed of the possibilities for trauma treatment when they deliver their rulings. They will have a genuine understanding that untreated childhood trauma can produce individuals who inflict harm. Domestic violence will be responded to at the earliest warnings and treatment will be strongly advised. This will make it possible for families to stay together.

- Divorce court judges will be informed about and sensitive to the possible trauma of divorce and recommend treatment to divorcing parents. This goes further than family court interventions, which already recommend conciliation therapy. Divorce lawyers will be trained in understanding the possible traumatization of divorce to children and adults alike, and will work in tandem with specialized therapists in divorce trauma, saving the nation's children from much confusion, pain, and difficulties. Trauma courses will be part of a lawyer's educational training.

- Insurance companies will save billions of dollars by revising their beliefs and extending benefits for trauma treatment. With the help of the government, they will invest in research on innovative techniques for healing trauma. They will understand the long-range impact of trauma on their clients and that the billions of dollars it costs them in medical care is often related to trauma. Disability insurances will have a clear stake in this new vision. Car accident victims, for example, will be automatically offered the chance to receive therapeutic treatment that allows them to discharge any residual traumatic hyperarousal and to reestablish their orienting and defensive responses.

- Paramedics will receive training in techniques that help lower panic attacks often experienced by people in emergency situations. The number of deaths on the way to the hospital will be significantly diminished and the exacerbation of symptoms due to psychological fear will be diminished.

- Doctors will be trained in all the possible symptomology of psychological trauma. It will help them accurately diagnose their patients' illnesses. More than 65 percent of medical appointments will be able to be diagnosed and treated for symptoms that will be understood as originating from stress responses.

- Hospital nurses will be trained in these techniques and will be able to alleviate considerable emotional suffering and physical pain. They will also be trained to use these techniques to alleviate their own symptoms from dealing with traumas and illnesses all day long. It will help them significantly reduce burnout and secondary traumatization.

- Emergency-room personnel will benefit from learning and applying these techniques more than anybody else. Emergency professions are among the most highly exposed to secondhand trauma of all the helping professions.

- Veterans returning from the battlefield will be offered counseling oriented toward processing the horrors they witnessed, suffered, or had to commit. Counseling will be made easily available to them and their families immediately and at later dates, as trauma may take years to emerge.

- Police officers will be trained in understanding the effects of traumatic shock on victims they are helping or interrogating. They will also be trained to recognize primary and secondary trauma symptoms in themselves and will be able to seek help for it without having to fear losing assignments. Their families will also be offered help for the ongoing stress of having loved ones whose lives are always on the line: the same for firefighters, disaster workers, prison guards, and so on.

- Once prisoners have served their mandated time, they would be freed only after going through trauma treatment. They will be made responsible for restitution, whenever possible, and given the chance to engage in work that can give them skills they can use when paroled. Our current terrifying and traumatizing prison culture leaves inmates more traumatized, angrier, and better trained in violence when they leave than when they arrived. (Ninety percent of hardcore criminals have histories of abuse in childhood. Clinical data on prisoners using the techniques described in Chapter 10 showed that it was much easier for them to take responsibility for their actions after they were treated for their own traumas.) Receiving acknowledgment for their own suffering and their terrible life experiences will make people more willing and better equipped to take responsibility for the suffering they inflicted on others.

- Through the media, communities hit by natural disasters will be offered information on where to get the necessary emotional help to process the traumatic impact of the event. Some of the healing from traumatic events will be done directly through the media, at a mass level, by showing videos on handling hyperarousal and on resiliency building.

- On the international scene, the international community will attempt to heal war traumas of whole nations. Preventive measures will be implemented before populations are returned to their cities or villages after massacres in which they have lost families and friends.

- The international media will present dictators who mount killing rampages as still polarized by trauma, thereby discrediting them in the eyes of their countrymen as positive and objective leaders. When possible, past traumas of these same countries will be unveiled and validated and solutions other than retaliatory massacres will be offered.

- All media members exposed to secondary trauma will be aware of the risks involved in their jobs and encouraged to seek help when they recognize traumatic symptoms in themselves, without risking the loss of important assignments. They will be exquisitely aware that any unresolved trauma might influence their choice of what is newsworthy and their style of coverage. They will also be aware that untreated personal traumas from their past might make them more vulnerable to biased reporting, job stress, and burnout.

- By the year 2040, as the information about trauma will have become as much a part of our daily life as information on cholesterol, fats, carbohydrates, or harmful exposure to the sun, people will not be held responsible for having been traumatized. They will be held responsible for not going for treatment and for actions that are by-products of the trauma vortex. The knowledge on trauma will be so widespread that ignorance of its effects will not be an excuse.

- Our judicial system will then be justifiably tough, once all other social structures (caring governmental policies, a well-informed and well-intended clergy, enlightened insurance companies) begin to support treatment for the emotional and physical health of traumatized people.

- Different media organizations will have sponsored well-funded rigorous research on the media's impact on society, including the copycat phenomenon, and will have taken a leading role in hosting public discourse on values and policies. They will serve the well being of the public by holding politicians and all public institutions responsible for demonstrating integrity in their public functions. They will have developed their own watchdogs.

MAKING TREMENDOUS CHANGES IN OUR WAY OF THINKING

Is it possible that a media, invited to help inaugurate these changes, would say no? As one journalist said: "It is true! Many journalists enter the field as idealists, wanting to uncover what's wrong and help to better society. I know I did . . . but I see now that leaving the business because I did not feel good about what I was doing was not the answer. I want to reenter it in a position and with people who want to take a leadership role in helping better our society."

What is really energizing about trauma, paradoxically, is that its healing is transformative for the individual as well as for society at large. Knowing how unresolved trauma engenders pessimism, cynicism, despair, and paralysis of the will, or desperate and uncontrolled acting out, we can understand how healing opens the door to hope, optimism, and the desire for creative and constructive action.

As the media's role has expanded, its responsibility has expanded. As we recognize the powerful influence of the mind, the media's responsibility to incorporate that reality fully into its presentation also expands. This is an invitation to put trauma, its impact, and the ability to be healed and transformed through it on the global agenda and to bring awareness to the effects of instantaneous communication.

The media mirrors society and society mirrors the media. This interrelationship takes on a more pointed meaning when related to trauma. Media members, trauma researchers, and clinicians are invited to engage in a dialogue on the expanding field of trauma knowledge. The media are the eyes, ears, and voice of our collective body. We must trust them and help them serve us well.

BIBLIOGRAPHY AND RESOURCES

Chapter References

Attias, R., and J. Goodwin. "Memories of Fear," in *Images of the Body in Trauma* (New York: Basic Books, 1997). In this chapter, Dr. Perry explores how the brain "stores and retrieves physiologic states, feelings, behaviors, and thoughts from traumatic events," and illustrates these issues with several case examples of traumatized children and adolescents.

Valent, Paul. "Introduction to Survival Strategies," in *From Survival to Fulfillment: A Framework for the Life-Trauma Dialectic* (New York: Bruner/Mazel, 1998). Paul Valent describes eight survival strategies in response to trauma—"stress responses which include specific adaptive and maladaptive, biological, psychological, and social constituents." Valent's survival strategies evolved as discrete phylogenetic templates to aid survival following specific stressors.

Van der Kolk, Bessel A., and Alexander C. McFarlane. "The Black Hole of Trauma" and

Van der Kolk, Bessel A., Alexander C. McFarlane, and Onno van der Hart. "A General Approach to Treatment of Posttraumatic Stress Disorder." These two chapters appear in *Traumatic Stress* (New York: The Guilford Press, 1996).

Articles

Alvarez-Conrad, J., Foa, E.B., and Zollner, L.A. "Peritraumatic Dissociative Experiences, Trauma Narratives, and Trauma Pathology," *Journal of Traumatic Stress* 15(1): 2002.

American Academy of Pediatrics, Committee on Communications. "Impact of music lyrics and rock music videos on children and youth," *Pediatrics* 98: 1996, pp. 1219–1221.

Brayne, Mark. "Even Journalists Need Counseling," BBC News Online (2001).

Dwairy, Marwan. "On Fear and Honor in the Conflict," *Indymedia Israel:* 2002. Found on the web at: www.indymedia.org.

Goode, Erica. "War Horrors Take a Toll on Reporters at the Front," *The New York Times.* September 11, 2002.

Grossman, Colonel Dave. "Trained to Kill," *Christianity Today,* August, 42(9): 1998, p. 40.

Haddon, W., Jr. "A Logical Framework for Categorizing Highway Safety Phenomena and Activity," *Journal of Trauma:* 1972.

Janet, Pierre. "Post-Traumatic Stress," *Journal of Traumatic Stress* 4(2): 1989.

Janet, Pierre. "L'Anesthesie Systematisee et la Dissociation des Phenomenes Psychologiques," *Revue Philosophique* 23(1): 1887.

Lester, Toby. "Oh, Gods!" *The Atlantic Monthly* 289(2): February 2002, pp. 37–45.

Levine, Peter A. "The Body as Healer: Transforming Trauma and Anxiety," published in a later version in *Panic: Origins, Insight, and Treatment,* edited by L.J. Schmidt and B. Warner. (Berkeley, California: North Atlantic Books, 2002), pp. 27–48. Levine's article covers the possibility of healing trauma through naturalistic methods.

Lindy, J.D., B.L. Green, and M. Grace. "Somatic Reenactment in the Treatment of Post-Traumatic Stress Disorder," *Psychotherapy and Psychosomatics* 57: 1992, pp. 180–186.

Marmar, C.R., D.S. Weiss, T.J. Metzler, and K. Delucchi. "Characteristics of Emergency Services Personnel Related to Peritraumatic Dissociations During Critical Incident Exposure," *American Journal of Psychiatry* 153(Fetschrift supplement): 1996, pp. 94–102.

Mehlum, Lars and Lars Weisaeth. "Predictors of Post-Traumatic Stress Reactions in Norwegian U.N. Peacekeepers Seven Years After Service," *Journal of Traumatic Stress* 15(1): 2001.

Perry, B.D., R.A. Pollard, T.L. Blakley, W.L. Baker, and D. Vigilante. "Childhood Trauma, the Neurobiology of Adaptation, and 'Use-Dependent' Development of the Brain: How 'States' Became 'Traits,'" *Infant Mental Health Journal* 16(4): 1995, pp. 271–291.

Report of the National Commission on Sleep Disorders, *USA Today,* January 1993: p. 63.

Ricchiardi, Sherry. "Coping with the Stress of Covering Horror," *American Journalism Review*: 2002.

Rosch, P. *"Is Job Stress America's Leading Adult Health Problem? A Commentary,"* *Business Insights* 87: 1991.

Ross, Gina. "The Trauma Vortex in Action Again in the Middle East," Various publications, 2001. Found on the web at: www.traumainstitute.org.

Rothschild, B. "A Shock Primer for the Body psychotherapist." *Energy and Character* 24(1): 1993, pp. 33–38.

Schouten, Dirk. "Trauma News Hurts Journalists Too," *UBC Thunderbird Online Magazine* IV: 2002.

Siegel, D.J. "Cognition, Memory, and Dissociation," *Child and Adolescent Psychiatric Clinics of North America* 5(2): 1996, pp. 509–536.

Skinner, B.F. "Teaching Machines," *Scientific American* 205(5): 1961, pp. 90–107.

Sorenson, Susan B. "Preventing Traumatic Stress: Public Health Approaches," *Journal of Traumatic Stress* 15(1): 2002.

Sykes, Mary W. *Networker,* July/August 1996.

Smyth, Frank. "Confronting the Horror," *American Journalism Review,* January/February, 1999.

Van der Hart, O. and K. Steele. "Relieving or Reliving Childhood Trauma? A Commentary on Miltenberg and Singer," *Theory and Psychology* 9(4): 1997, pp. 533–540.

Van der Kolk, B.A. "The Body Keeps the Score: Memory and the Evolving Psychobiology of Post-Traumatic Stress," *Harvard Review of Psychiatry* 1(5): 1994, pp. 253–265. This article provides an excellent and very clear description of many aspects of memory for traumatic events, and it includes extensive references.

Yehuda, R., M.H. Teicher, R. Levengood, R. Trestman, and L.J. Siever. "Cortisol Regulation in Post-Traumatic Stress Disorder and Major Depression: A Chronobiological Analysis," *Biological Psychiatry* 40: 1996, pp. 79–88.

Books

Alexander, Gerda. *Eutony: The Holistic Discovery of the Total Person* (New York: Felix Morrow Publishers, 1986).

Allen, Jon G. *Coping with Trauma: A Guide to Self-Understanding* (Washington, D.C.: American Psychiatric Press, 1995).

Ben Gad, Yitschak. *Politics Lies and Videotape: 3,000 Question & Answers on the Mideast Crisis* (New York: Shapolsky Publishers, Inc., 1991).

Best, Joel. *Random Violence: How We Talk About New Crimes and New Victims* (Berkeley and Los Angeles, CA: University of California Press, 1999).

Bloch, G. *Body and Self: Elements of Human Biology, Behavior, and Health* (Los Altos, CA: William Kaufman, 1985).

Brown, Daniel P., Alan W. Scheflin, and D. Corydon Hammond. *Memory, Trauma Treatment, and the Law* (New York: W.W. Norton & Company, 1998).

Bull, Chris, and Sam Erman. *At Ground Zero* (New York: Thunder's Mouth Press, 2002).

Cantor, Joanne. *"Mommy, I'm Scared": How TV and Movies Frighten Children and What We Can Do to Protect Them* (Fort Washington, PA: Harvest Books, 1999).

Cote, William E., and Roger Simpson. *Covering Violence* (New York: Columbia University Press, 1999).

Damasio, Antonio R. *Descartes' Error: Emotion, Reason, and the Human Brain* (New York: Avon Books, 1994).

Danieli, Yael. *Sharing the Front Line and the Back Hills* (Amityville, NY: Baywood Publishing Company, Inc., 2002).

Figley, Charles R. *Compassion Fatigue: Coping with Secondary Traumatic Stress Disorder in Those Who Treat the Traumatized* (New York: Brunner/Mazel, 1995).

Figley, Charles, Brian E. Bride, and Nicholas Mazza. *Death and Trauma: The Traumatology of Grieving* (New York: Taylor & Francis, 1997).

Flint, Garry A. *Emotional Freedom: Techniques for Dealing with Psychological, Emotional, and Physical Distress* (British Columbia: Neosol Terric Enterprises, 1999).

Foa, Edna. *Treating the Trauma of Rape: Cognitive-Behavioral Therapy for PTSD* (New York: Guilford Press, 2001).

Gabler, Neal. *Life, the Movie: How Entertainment Conquered Reality* (New York: Vintage Books, 1998).

Garbarino, James. *Lost Boys: Why Our Sons Turn Violent and How We Can Save Them* (New York: Brunner/Mazel, 1999).

Gist, Richard, and Bernard Lubin. *Response to Disasters: Psychosocial, Community, and Ecological Approaches* (New York: Brunner/Mazel, 1999).

Gordon, Norman S., Norman L. Farberow, and Carl A. Maida. *Children and Disasters* (New York: Brunner/Mazel, 1999).

Greenwald, Ricky. *Eye Movement Desensitization Reprocessing (EMDR) in Child and Adolescent Therapy* (Northwale, NJ: Jason Aronson, 1999).

Heller, Diane Poole, with Laurence S. Heller. *Crash Course: A Self-Healing Guide to Auto Accident Trauma & Recovery* (Berkeley, CA: North Atlantic Books, 2001).

Herman, Judith. *Trauma and Recovery* (New York: Basic Books, 1992).

Hight, Joe, and Frank Smyth. *Tragedies and Journalists.* Dart Center for Journalism and Trauma, published in the *Hearst Newspapers* and the *Houston Chronicle*, 2002.

Jamieson, Kathleen Hall, and Paul Waldman. *The Press Effect: Politicians, Journalists, and the Stories That Shape the Political World* (New York: Oxford University Press, 2003[publication pending]).

Johanson, Greg, and Ron Kurtz. *Grace Unfolding: Psychotherapy in the Spirit of the Tao-te Ching* (New York: Bell Tower, 1991).

Johnson, Kendall, and Charles Figley. *Trauma in the Lives of Children: Crisis and Stress Management Techniques for Counselors, Teachers, and Other Professionals* (Alameda, CA: Hunter House, 1998).

Kurtz, Howard. *Spin Cycle: How the White House and the Media Manipulate the News* (New York: Touchstone, 1998).

Lapham, Lewish H. *Understanding Media* (Cambridge, MA: First MIT Press, 1st edition, 1994).

LeDoux, Joseph. *The Emotional Brain: The Mysterious Underpinnings of Emotional Life* (New York: Simon & Schuster, 1996).

Levine, Peter A. *Waking the Tiger: Healing Trauma* (Berkeley, CA: North Atlantic Books, 1992).

Lovett, Joan, and Francine Shapiro. *Small Wonders: Healing Childhood Trauma with EMDR* (London: Free Press, 1992).

Luria, Alexander R. *Working Brain: An Introduction to Neuropsychology* (New York: Basic Books, 1973).

Matsakis, Aphrodite. *Survivor Guilt* (Oakland, CA: New Harbinger Publications, 1999).

Matsakis, Aphrodite. *I Can't Get Over It: A Handbook for Trauma Survivors* (Oakland, CA: New Harbinger Publications, 1996).

Melman, Yossi, and Dan Reviv. *Behind the Uprising* (New York: Greenwood Press, 1989).

Nesse, R., M.D., and G. Williams, Ph.D. *Why We Get Sick* (New York: Vintage Books, 1996), p. 212.

Nydell, K (Omar) Margaret. *Understanding Arabs: A Guide for Westerners* (Yarmouth, ME: Intercultural Press, Inc., 1996).

Ochberg, Frank. *Post-Traumatic Therapy and Victims of Violence* (New York: Brunner/Mazel, 1988).

Ochberg, Frank. *Victims of Terrorism* (Boulder, CO: Westview Press, 1982).

Pavlov, I.P. *Conditioned Reflexes* (New York: Dover, 1960).

Perry, Bruce. *Maltreated Children: Experience, Brain Development and the Next Generation* (New York: W.W. Norton & Company, 2003[publication pending]).

Pert, Candace, and Deepak Chopra. *Molecules of Emotion: Why You Feel the Way You Feel* (New York: Simon & Schuster, 1997).

Raviv, Dan, and Yossi Melman. *Friends in Deed: Inside the U.S.—Israel Alliance* (New York: Hyperion, 1994).

Rosenbloom, Dana, and Mary Beth Williams. *Life After Trauma: A Workbook for Healing* (New York: Guilford Press, 1999).

Rothschild, Babette. *The Body Remembers: The Psychophysiology of Trauma and Trauma Treatment* (New York: W.W. Norton & Company, 2001).

Saakvitne, Karen W., and Laurie Anne Pearlman. *Transforming the Pain: A Workbook on Vicarious Traumatization* (New York: W.W. Norton & Company, 1996).

Saigh, Phillip, and Douglass J. Bremner. *Post-traumatic Stress Disorder: A Comprehensive Text* (Boston: Allyn & Bacon, 1999).

Sanders, Catherine M. *Grief: The Mourning After: Dealing with Adult Bereavement.* (New York: John Wily & Sons, 1999).

Sarna, Igal. *The Man Who Fell into a Puddle* (Tel Aviv: Sifrei Chemed, Pantheon Books, 2002).

Schore, Allan N. *Affect Regulation and the Origin of the Self: The Neurobiology of Emotional Development* (Hillsdale, NJ: Lawrence Erlbaum Associates, 1994).

Shapiro, Francine. *Eye Movement Desensitization and Reprocessing* (New York: Guilford Press, 1995).

Siegel, Daniel J. *The Developing Mind* (New York: Guilford Press, 1999).

Stamm, B. Hudnall. *Secondary Traumatic Stress: Self-care Issues for Clinicians, Researchers, and Educators* (Lutherville, MD: Sidran Press, 1996).

Staub, Ervin. *The Roots of Evil* (Cambridge: Cambridge University Press, 1989).

Swedo, Susan, and Henrietta Leonard. *It's NOT All in Your Head* (San Francisco: Harper San Francisco, 1996).

Taylor, Eugene. *Shadow Culture* (Washington, D.C.: Counterpoint, 1999).

Terr, Lenore. *Unchained Memories: True Stories of Traumatic Memories Lost and Found* (New York: Basic Books, 1994).

Tinker, Robert H., Sandra Wilson, and Robbie Dutton. *Through the Eyes of a Child: EMDR with Children* (New York: W.W. Norton & Company, 1999).

Valent, Paul. *Trauma and Fulfillment Therapy: A Holist Framework: Pathways to Fulfillment* (New York: Taylor & Francis, 1999).

Van der Kolk, Bessel A. *Psychological Trauma* (Washington, D.C.: American Psychiatric Press, 1987).

Van der Kolk , Bessel A., A.C. MacFarlane, and L. Weisaeth. *Traumatic Stress: A Psychological and Research Perspective on Trauma* (New York: Guilford Press, 1996).

Williams, Ruth M., William Yule, and Stephen Joseph. *Understanding Post Traumatic Stress: A Psychosocial Perspective on PTSD and Treatment* (New York: John Wiley & Sons, 1997).

Worden, J. William. *Children and Grief: When a Parent Dies* (New York: Guilford Press, 1996).

Yehuda, Rachel, Ph.D. *Psychological Trauma* (Washington, D.C. and London: American Psychiatric Press, 1999).

Organizations and Websites

AMERICAN ACADEMY OF PEDIATRICS

An organization representing the nation's pediatricians. Provides information about the impact of media on children, materials on media education, and publishes brochures on television and the family.

P.O. Box 927
Elk Grove Village, IL 60009-0927
Phone: (847) 434-4000
Fax: (847) 434-8000
http://www.aap.org

CENTER FOR MEDIA EDUCATION

A national nonprofit organization dedicated to creating a quality electronic media culture for children and youth, families, and the community.

2120 L Street, NW, Suite 200
Washington, DC 20037
Phone: (202) 331-7833
Fax: (202) 331-7841
Email: cme@cme.org
http://www.cme.org

CENTER FOR MEDIA LITERACY

Publishes both text and media resources for use in classroom media study activities and is dedicated to the promotion of media literacy in schools, churches, and other community programs concerned with the effects of mass media on youth and families.

3101 Ocean Park Boulevard, #200
Santa Monica, CA 90405
Phone: (310) 581-0260
Fax: (310) 581-0270
Email: cml@medialit.org
http://www.medialit.org

CENTER FOR MEDIA AND PUBLIC AFFAIRS

The center tracks crime coverage; in 1996 it found that TV crime had quadrupled, while real-world rates dropped, and that O.J. Simpson received more coverage than all the presidential candidates combined.

2100 L St., NW, Suite 300
Washington, DC 20037
Contact: Jeanne Maynard, Director of Administration
Daniel Amundson, Research Director
Phone: (202) 223-2942
Fax: (202) 872-4014
Email: cmpamm@aol.com
http://www.cmpa.com

CRITICAL VIEWING PROJECT

The Family & Community Critical Viewing Project is a first-of-its-kind partnership of the National Parent Teacher Association, Cable in the Classroom, and the National Cable Television Association. It was launched in 1994 to address concerns about television and the impact of television violence and commercialism on children.

1724 Massachusetts Ave., NW
Washington, DC 20036
Contact: Hubert Jessup
Phone: (202) 775-3629
http://www.kuglin.com/theacriticalaviewingaproject.htm

DART CENTER FOR JOURNALISM & TRAUMA

The Dart Center is a global network of journalists, journalism educators, and health professionals dedicated to improving media coverage of trauma, conflict, and tragedy. The Center also addresses the consequences of such coverage for those working in journalism.

Department of Communication
102 Communications Bldg.
Box 353740
University of Washington
Seattle, WA 98195-3740
Phone: (206) 616-3223
Fax: (206) 543-9285
Email: info@dartcenter.org
http://www.dartcenter.org

THE INTERNATIONAL TRAUMA-HEALING INSTITUTE

Established to promote peace at the community, national, and international levels by bringing global awareness to the nature of trauma, its costs, and its link to violence, the institute's goals are to promote awareness of existing resources and techniques for coping with and healing trauma and facilitating the availability of these resources to the global community, and to promote the media's role in helping to heal trauma.

269 S. Lorraine Blvd.
Los Angeles, CA 90004
Contact: Gina Ross
Phone: (323) 954-1400
Fax: (323) 935-8417
Email: info@traumainstitute.org
http://www.traumainstitute.org

THE JUST THINK FOUNDATION

Established to promote critical thinking about popular media. The Foundation addresses the fundamental issues behind how traditional and interactive media influence the behavior of young people. *Just Think* is creating messages that evoke consciousness about media. *Just Think* is applying these messages to spark critical thinking about the media young people experience every day.

39 Mesa St., Suite 106
Presidio Park
San Francisco, CA 94129
Phone: (415) 561-2900
Fax: (415) 561-2901
Email: think@justthink.org
http://www.justthink.org

KIDSNET

The only computerized clearinghouse devoted to children's TV, video, radio, and audio programming. Publishes monthly media guides, quarterly media news, and study guides.

6856 Eastern Avenue, NW, Suite 208
Washington, DC 20012
Phone: (202) 29-1400
Fax: (202) 882-7315
Email: kidsnet@kidsnet.org
http://www.kidsnet.org

MADD (MOTHERS AGAINST DRUNK DRIVING)

MADD is a nonprofit grassroots organization with more than 600 chapters nationwide. MADD's mission is to stop drunk driving, support the victims of this violent crime, and prevent underage drinking.

511 East John Carpenter Freeway, Suite 700
Irving, TX 75062
Phone: (800) 438-6233
Fax: (972) 869-2206/ (972) 869-2207
http://www.madd.org

THE MEDIA FOUNDATION

A global network of artists, activists, writers, pranksters, students, educators, and entrepreneurs who want to advance the new social activist movement of the information age. They are widely known for their *Adbusters* publication and TV commercials.

1243 West 7th Avenue
Vancouver, BC
V6H 1B7, Canada
Phone: (604) 736-9401
Fax: (604) 737-6021
Email: info@adbusters.org
http://www.adbusters.org/information/foundation

MEDIA MATTERS

The national media education campaign of the American Academy of Pediatrics is committed to the attainment of optimal physical, mental and social health, and well being for all infants, children, adolescents, and young adults.

141 Northwest Point Boulevard
Elk Grove Village, IL 60007-1098
Phone: (847) 434-4000
Fax: (847) 434-8000
Email: mediamatters@aap.org
http://www.aap.org/advocacy/mediamatters.htm

MEDIASCOPE

Mediascope is a national, nonprofit research and policy organization for the promotion of issues of social relevance within the entertainment industry.

12711 Ventura Boulevard, Suite 440
Studio City, CA 91604
Phone: (818) 508-2080
Fax: (818) 508-2088
Email: facts@mediascope.org
http://www.mediascope.org

THE NATIONAL CHILDREN'S COALITION

This is the place to find the latest and most complete information about kids and teens—and the most complete listing of great places and projects for children and youth on the World Wide Web.

Streetcats Foundation
267 Lester Avenue, Suite 104
Oakland, CA 94606
Phone: (866) 227-3709
Email: helpingyouth@yahoo.com
http://www.child.net

THE NATIONAL COALITION ON TELEVISION VIOLENCE

Website for the NCTV, leading advocates for the V-chip and other tools to empower parents to control the amount of media violence to which children are exposed.

http://www.nctvv.org

NATIONAL INSTITUTE ON MEDIA AND THE FAMILY

Provides research, information, and resources about the impact of media on children so parents can make better media choices for their children. A special feature is the institute's report card and guide for video and computer games.

606 24th Avenue South, Suite 606
Minneapolis, MN 55454
Phone: (888) 672-5437 / (612) 672-5437
http://www.mediafamily.org

NATIONAL PTA—CHILDREN FIRST & MEDIA PROGRAMMING

A nonprofit association of parents, educators, students, and other citizens active in their schools and communities.

330 N. Wabash Ave., Suite 2100
Chicago, IL 60611
Phone: (312) 670-6782 / (800) 307-4PTA
Fax: (312) 670-6783
http://www.pta.org

NATIONAL TELEMEDIA COUNCIL (NTC)

A professional media literacy organization promoted through the publication *Telemedium: The Journal of Media Literacy* (http://danenet. danenet.org/ntc). The Council conducts workshops for teachers, parents, and others on teaching about the media, understanding media, and managing television and the family. *Media & You* offers simple media literacy exercises with no need for video equipment. The *Best of Teacher Ideas* is a collection of practical applications from Telemedia.

1922 University Avenue
Madison, WI 53726
Phone: (608) 218-1182
Fax: (608) 218-1183
Email: NTelemedia@aol.com
http://www.nationaltelemediacouncil.org

THE SMART PARENT'S GUIDE TO KID'S TV

Written by Dr. Milton Chen of PBS station KQED in San Francisco, a longtime advocate for quality children's television, this is a timely and practical guide that helps parents take control of the television. Includes useful tips and activities to enhance the benefits and less the ill effects of TV.

P.O. Box 927
Elk Grove Village, IL 60009-0927
Phone: (847) 434-4000
Fax: (847) 434-8000
http://www.aap.org/family/smarttv.htm

THE TELEVISION PROJECT

An educational organization to help parents understand how television affects their families and community, and to propose alternatives that foster positive emotional, cognitive, and spiritual development within families and communities.

2311 Kimball Place
Silver Spring, MD 20910
Phone: (301) 588-4001

Contact: Annamrie Pluhar, Executive Director
Email: info@tvp.org
http://www.tvp.org

THE WORKING REPORTER

A toolkit for working journalists of all stripes, which includes language translators, public records searching, and best of all, message boards and chat functions where reporters can discuss pressing issues with one another.

Email: workingreporter@workingreporter.com
http://www.workingreporter.com

Healing Methods Online

EMOTIONAL FREEDOM TECHNIQUE

www.emofree.com
ACEP: www.energypsych.org
Chilel Qigong: www.chilel.com

EYE MOVEMENT DESENSITIZATION AND REPROCESSING (EMDR)

P.O. Box 140824
Austin, TX 78714-0824
Phone: (512) 302-9943
Fax: (512) 451-0329
Contact: Robbie Dunton
Email: rdunton@emdr.com

SOMATIC EXPERIENCING

Foundation For Human Enrichment
P.O. Box 1872
Lyons, CO 80540
Phone: (303) 823-9524
Fax: (303) 823-9520
Email: ergos1@earthlink.net
http://www.traumahealing.com

TRAUMATIC INCIDENT REDUCTION (TIR)

http://www.healing-arts.org/tir
Email: Gerald.French@post.harvard.edu
Phone: (800) 499-2751 (U.S. Canada)
(816) 468-4945 (International)
Fax: (816) 468-6656
Email: tira@tir.org
http://www.tir.org

Articles And Studies Available Online

"Open Questions on the Correlation Between Television and Violence,"
by Jonathan Vos Post
A first-rate summation of competing theories on the connections
between television and violence.

http://www.magicdragon.com/EmeraldCity/Nonfiction/socphil.html

"Trained to Kill," by Colonel David Grossman
Colonel Grossman lays out his compelling but controversial argument that modern media violence replicates the techniques used by
the world's militaries to train soldiers to kill.

http://www.christianity.net/ct/8T9/8T9030.html.

"V-Chip TV Rating System Study," by Professor Dale Kunkel, University of California at Santa Barbara, and "The Entertainment Media
and Public Health" are among many studies supported by the Kaiser
Family Foundation and can be found on their website:

www.kff.org.

Appendix

Tips for Parents Dealing with Children and Media

The following article is presented both for the benefit of parents looking for ways to deal with their children's relationship to the media, and for the media's awareness:

"Beyond Blame," by Elizabeth Thoman, was first published in the Center for Media Literacy's *Media &Values.*

Beyond the blame, beyond the debate, are human beings—children, young people, and adults of all ages—who are daily bombarded with violent images from the media and popular culture.

The parameters of this problem are complex and interrelated. There are First Amendment concerns as well as public policies resulting from the deregulation of the media industry during the Reagan years. And as Walter Wink so eloquently writes, "violence is the very stuff of our fundamental mythologies, including the myth of the American West."

While Hollywood may feed these myths, Hollywood did not start them. Nor can Washington legislate them under the rug. Violence cannot be sanitized out of our culture even if gruesome and gratuitous violence becomes "politically incorrect" in popular entertainment. Over the decades, we've seen the media industry "self-censor" many creative ideas and images from the Amos 'n Andy stereotype of African-Americans to the use of alcohol, cigarettes, and even hard drugs. Excessive violence can be added to the list.

But there will still be violence in life, and in the media, because there is tragedy and evil in the world and human nature has its shadow side. There is also grinding poverty and addiction and meaninglessness, which create a seedbed for violence as way for some to cope with injustice. Such violence will find its way into the news and into the storylines of both high art and popular culture.

Nevertheless violence is a major social problem today and we must find workable solutions to prevent its further growth. Years of research and work on this issue show clearly that media literacy must be a necessary component of any effective effort at violence prevention, for both individuals and society as a whole.

Programs of media literacy cannot replace society's storytellers' share of responsibility for our cultural environment. But parents and caretakers have a role as well. Here are five ways media literacy can contribute to lessening the impact and incidence of violence in our world:

1. Reducing exposure to media violence

Educating parents and caretakers about the issue and helping them to develop and enforce age-appropriate viewing limits. How many times have you been in a violent R-rated movie and seen children there? Adults must come to realize that media violence today is different than when they were growing up. Parent organizations, churches, and social workers need to get the message out that too much media violence may truly harm young children. Programs of media literacy for parents can help.

2. Changing the impact of violent images that are seen

Deconstructing the techniques used to stage violent scenes and decoding the various depictions of violence in different genres—news, cartoons, drama, sports, and music. It is important for children to learn early on the difference between reality and fantasy and to know how costumes and camera angles and special effects can fool or mesmerize them. Media literacy activities need to be integrated into every learning environment—school, church or temple, Scouts and clubs.

3. Locating and exploring alternatives to storytelling that highlights violence

Schools, libraries, and families (as well as grandparents) need to have access to books and tapes that provide positive role models to help counterbalance the actions and attitudes of today's "superheroes." Through media literacy classes, parents can also learn to transform undesirable images from popular culture into opportunities for positive modeling. One father, for example, let his child watch *Teenage Mutant Ninja Turtles,* but only if the child would imagine a fifth turtle named "Gandhi." Afterwards they had a great discussion on how "Ninja Gandhi" might get the Turtles out of trouble without resorting to violence!

4. Uncovering and challenging the cultural, economic, political, and psychological supports

Media violence, greed, competition, dominance, and structural poverty, as well as the personal ways we may each be contributing to the creation or perpetuation of a mediated culture of violence, need to be challenged. We must remember the root of our cherished freedom of speech was not to protect creativity at any cost but to challenge the political and economic status quo.

Media literacy empowers its participants to ask hard questions of themselves, of others, and of society by applying the principles of critical thinking to experiences that look like "mindless entertainment." Indeed, the systemic analysis provided through media literacy can provide a learning curve to an informed and knowledgeable media activism.

5. Breaking the cycle of blame and promoting informed and rational public debate

Talking about these issues in schools, community, civic gatherings, religious groups, and the media itself. The grim reality of our current situation demands that we ask two fundamental questions of ourselves as a society:

- What kind of culture do we want our children to grow up in?

- Can we continue contributing, through our choices, to allow profit from products that might be contributing to a social condition that endangers public safety? Indeed, an informed public is less vulnerable to extremist views or actions.

In 1993, the Center for Media Literacy developed "Beyond Blame: Challenging Violence in the Media," an innovative community education program, based on the principles of media literacy, to directly address the issues of violence in the media.

[Center for Media Literacy, copyright 1993.]

Resources for Children

Talk to Someone Who Can Help, a brochure about psychotherapy and choosing a psychologist from the American Psychological Association (750 First St. NE, Washington, DC 20002-4242) can be ordered free of charge. Call (800) 964-2000. Contact the APA Practice Directorate at (202) 336-5800 for the name and telephone number of your state psychological association. These associations, along with city and county psychological associations can refer you to psychologists in your area. They may also be able to put you in touch with other local organizations and groups that help victims of disasters and other traumatic events.

Local chapters of the American Red Cross may be able to direct you to additional resources. Check your local telephone directory for the nearest chapter.

National Organization for Victims Assistance
1757 Park Rd., NW
Washington, D.C. 20010
Phone: toll-free: (800) TRY-NOVA
D.C. Metropolitan Area: (202) 232-6682.

Emotional Reactions to Disasters, available from the University of Illinois Cooperative Extension Service.

Human Enrichment Foundation available at www.traumahealing.com.

Contact www.traumainstitute.org or ginaross@traumainstitute.com for additional information on media and the healing of trauma as well as to:

Links and resources to other trauma sites and resources
Information on the International Trauma-Healing Institute
To participate in the global healing of trauma and the media
To contribute trauma articles, links and resources to the websites:
www.traumainstitute.org
www.traumahealing.org

Free Newsletter

KEEP UP TO DATE ON TRAUMA ISSUES TODAY!

Readers receive a free subscription to our online newsletter.

Go to www.traumainstitute.org and sign up now!

Thank you for your contribution to the International Trauma-Healing Institute (ITI).

All proceeds from the sale of this book go directly to ITI to support its goal of helping heal trauma worldwide.

With your help, the International Trauma-Healing Institute fulfills its mission of promoting peace at the community, national, and international level by bringing awareness to trauma as a root cause of conflict and violence and to the resources available for trauma's resolution and healing.

We invite your continued participation. Together we can promote and encourage healing around the world. For more information on ITI's activities and to learn about the various ways you can help, visit us at www.traumainstitute.org.

All financial contributions are tax-deductible and can be made to the "International Trauma-Healing Institute" at:

International Trauma-Healing Institute
269 S. Lorraine Blvd
Los Angeles, CA 90004
Gina Ross
Founder and Chairperson
International Trauma-Healing Institute

GINA ROSS, MFCC, is the founder and chair of the International Trauma-Healing Institute in the United States and the co-founder of the Israeli Trauma Center in Jerusalem. She specializes in trauma and has been involved in the understanding and treatment of trauma since 1990. She is trained in cognitive, behavioral, and somatic treatment approaches and is certified in the more innovative techniques of Somatic Experiencing (SE), Eye Movement Desensitization and Reprocessing (EMDR), Thought Field Therapy (TFT), and Traumatic Incident Reduction (TIR). She was the founder and chair for seven years of the Cross-Cultural Committee under the Los Angeles, California, Association of Marriage, Family, and Child Therapists (MFCT) and serves multi-cultural clientele from over 50 countries in her cross-cultural practice.

Ross is a faculty member and teacher/trainer for the Foundation for Human Enrichment; she has presented at international conferences as well as appearing on radio and television. An expert on the impact of trauma on individuals, communities, groups, and nations, Ross sees a major role for the media. She and her institute have undertaken the goal of putting and keeping the issue of trauma on the global agenda, and developing resources and collaborating with organizations to further the healing of trauma at the community, national, and international level. Currently, she is working with Israeli and Palestinian society, and particularly the media, to bring about understanding of the role of trauma and the political trauma vortex in Middle Eastern politics. She is developing a national model that can be applied to other regions as well. She is the published author of several articles. *Beyond the Trauma Vortex: The Media's Role in Healing Fear, Terror, and Violence* is her first book. Gina Ross can be reached at: ginaross@traumainstitute.org.